God Loves Single Moms

Practical Help for Finding
Confidence, Strength, and Hope

Teresa Whitehurst

Revell

a division of Baker Publishing Group
Grand Rapids, Michigan

Published by Revell
a division of Baker Publishing Group
P.O. Box 6287, Grand Rapids, MI 49516-6287
www.revellbooks.com

Printed in the United States of America

Library of Congress Cataloging-in-Publication Data
Whitehurst, Teresa, 1954–
    God loves single moms : practical help for finding confidence, strength, and hope / Teresa Whitehurst.
        p.   cm.
    Includes bibliographical references.
    ISBN 978-0-8007-3277-6 (pbk. : alk. paper)
    1. Single mothers—Religious life. 2. Christian women—Religious life. 3. Motherhood—Religious aspects—Christianity. 4. Single mothers. 5. Motherhood. I. Title.
BV4529.18.W47 2010
248.8′431—dc22   2010022466

10 11 12 13 14 15 16   7 6 5 4 3 2 1

God Loves Single Moms is dedicated to all single mothers who want to give their children the best of everything, and who sometimes need reminders to give themselves the same priority in life. As the old country saying goes, "If Mama ain't happy, ain't *nobody* happy." So single moms, let's get happy! I wish you all the best as you reevaluate and recraft your personal and family lives—for your children's sake, yes, but for *your* benefit as well.

I also dedicate this book to my children and grandchildren with great love and gratitude.

Contents

Acknowledgments

First and foremost, I would like to thank God for providing the love, encouragement, and unending patience that I needed while researching and writing *God Loves Single Moms*. In addition, I'd like to express my heartfelt appreciation to the following people.

I'm so grateful to the entire team at Baker Publishing Group, especially Vicki Crumpton and Wendy Wetzel, who exhibited remarkable gentleness and tact while editing the manuscript and receiving my last-minute additions. Many thanks also to Janelle Mahlman for helping me to refine the book's title and focus and who, along with Vicki, graciously heard and discussed my many ideas and suggestions.

In addition to my single-mom friends, many psychotherapy clients who've been single mothers at one time or another have provided me with insights that I never would have gained from education and training alone. Only those who have been through the struggles yet appreciate the joys of single motherhood can fully understand our unique needs, "lessons learned," and blessings.

My heartfelt thanks go to the two daughters I love so dearly, Isadora and Sascha, for being supportive of my writing. I feel grateful also for my son-in-law, Peter; my grandson, Luca; and the newest member of our family, my granddaughter, Rilo Rose. I take great joy in seeing Sascha and Peter nurture their own children with such care and dedication. Thank you all for being my family.

I'd also like to acknowledge my wonderful coach Gail Mc-Meekin, LICSW, author of inspiring books such as *The 12 Secrets of Highly Creative Women: A Portable Memoir*. Gail, I'm so glad I found your website (www.creativesuccess.com) and you!

Introduction

You're all grown up with children of your own. You have daily responsibilities, to-do lists, and a multitude of concerns. On good days you handle everything with ease, but on challenging days you may feel that it's all too much, or that you've become all work and no play. After rushing around the house getting your children off to school, you dash in to work, spilling coffee on your clean blouse while stuck in traffic and suddenly remembering that you forgot to take the clothes out of the dryer. You may fall into bed after taking care of everybody and everything without noticing or even caring that you never got the dishes washed or that your silken nightie is on backward.

Rest assured, it comes with the territory. Mothers, and single mothers especially, juggle so many things that fatigue and dreariness can sneak up on us before we know it. Who cares, after a full day of work, cleaning, bill paying, cooking dinner, and getting the kids to finish their homework or to just stop whining, if your nails are chipped or your clothes are piled on the floor? Where's the energy to even remember that you're a person too and that somewhere inside you lives the little girl you once were?

This book is for the mother, the woman, the CEO, and yes, the little girl in you. It's essential that you stop, reflect, and ask God for the daily (sometimes hourly) strength to care for your children, maintain your household, tackle problems, and find ways to regularly rejuvenate your body and spirit.

In every one of you now reading these words is an inner child who needs just as much (sometimes more) of the following as your children do: guidance, attention, limit setting, encouragement, and yes, even treats now and then. As you develop your skills, insightfulness, and resilience as a mother, you'll become better able to understand and care for the little girl inside you as well. The more happy and energetic *she* is, the more happy and energetic *you'll* be as a mother.

Accentuating the Positive

When I became a single mother, I realized that I was treading on new territory. In the neighborhood and time in which I grew up, very few children were "children of divorce," and they were careful not to mention it. The term "single mother" was rarely used to describe a woman with children who'd become single again through divorce; usually she was referred to as a "divorcee" or "divorced woman." The former term conjured up shady connotations of a wild partyer, while the latter term suggested that the woman was a victim of abandonment. Mothers whose husbands had died were referred to as "widows," an accurate term but one that emphasized their loss, not their continuing roles as parents.

Prior to the last few decades, few positive words or images were used to reflect the possibility of a happy, well-adjusted, and spiritually sound single-mother family. Not surprisingly, there was very little awareness or media attention regarding the specific needs of single mothers. A "divorcee" didn't sound as if she needed (or maybe even deserved) attention, respect, and guidance, and a "widow" was given sympathy at first, but not the kind of ongoing attention and help she needed in her new role as a single mother.

While we don't have children with the wish to parent them solo, when we do become single mothers we have the responsibility to learn the ropes of this highly demanding and highly fulfilling role. Thankfully, our children don't have to bear the same burdens they once did: because kids raised in single-parent homes aren't such a minority today, they no longer feel stigmatized or "different" from their peers and tend to be matter-of-fact about their family structure. This is echoed in today's generally more open and supportive stance toward single parenting.

However, we as single mothers do need to recognize that it isn't easy to raise a child alone, and though we don't have a partner right now, we need not try to "do it all by ourselves." We can rely on God, and we can recognize that it's okay to reach out to other people for help and support. A spiritual, interpersonal, and practical "team approach" to single motherhood, as will be described in this book, is far wiser than trying to go it alone—for the sake of your well-being as well as your child's.

Why Single Mothers Need God

Single mothers are treasured by God and are entrusted with the important job of caring for, watching over, and guiding their children. This fact may be missed, at times, due to the emphasis on

---

The Bright Side of Single Mothering

When you're a single parent, your child doesn't have to hear arguing or feel the tension of "silent treatments" between parents at home (of course you'll want to monitor your conversations by telephone and at visitation/trade-off times). This freedom from witnessing or having to get involved in stressful adult conflicts can provide a more secure foundation for your child's emotional and cognitive development.

---

married parents in many Christian parenting books and classes as well as in many churches. Taking to heart the omission of references to single mothers can give a single mom a feeling of being left out or that hers isn't a "real" family. As a result she may stop attending church or take a very quiet, backseat role. She may even hesitate to pray for what she needs with the confidence that God values single- and married-parent families equally.

This subtle lack of confidence that her prayers will be answered is hazardous, because if anyone needs faith, it's a single mother. Single moms need to feel free to pray daily, hourly, or "without ceasing" when the demands on them are high and their energies are running low.

On the Wings of Eagles

The old bumper sticker states, "God is my co-pilot," but a more realistic and helpful way of viewing God is as your air traffic controller. A co-pilot helps the pilot fly the plane, takes over as needed, and so on. It's tempting to let go of the controls, thinking that if we don't handle something, God will. However, this is not how life works. If we get into debt because we're afraid to open our bills or confront an unpleasant reality, we shouldn't assume that God will fix our credit report. We must not fall into the trap of becoming passive, especially when we're stressed. Certainly we can and should pray for strength and guidance, but we will suffer if we don't stay alert and take action as well.

As a single parent, you must constantly make decisions, some of them split-second and some long-range, adjusting your course as you go. I'm absolutely not going to advise a single mother (or anyone, for that matter) to just pray and leave it at that. I will admit that during difficult times in my life, I've done the very thing I'm urging you not to do: I've viewed God as my co-pilot, as somebody who'll navigate through challenging situations even if I let go of the controls.

What that attitude led to, although I didn't realize it at the time, was a sense that everything would be fine no matter how I "drove" because God would correct any wrong turns that I made. Faith is essential, and we need to know that we can seek God's guidance at all times—but that's very different from assuming that when we get tired or run into obstacles, we can just leave the driving to God.

As a young single mom I certainly needed to feel that God was with me—this was an improvement over feeling that I'd made mistakes and was all alone in the world—but the idea of God as co-pilot often resulted in my thinking that I didn't have to think too deeply or carefully. I sometimes failed to predict the longer-term effects of my decisions or recognize that I needed to learn new skills or simply *do* something.

When you begin to see God as your air traffic controller, you'll notice a new level of challenge and maybe even anxiety, but eventually you'll develop a higher level of competence and confidence. An air traffic controller alerts the pilot to weather and airport conditions ahead and guides the pilot for safe takeoffs and landings. The pilot must remain alert and "on task" yet always keep hearing and heeding the controller's words.

God sees what you are doing in your life from a higher level than you possibly can, and—very importantly—he truly knows and understands you: your current skills, your level of experience, and the areas in which you need to improve. With the empathy of a loving parent, God also understands you in light of your past experiences: what you've achieved, strived for, and coped with in your life thus far.

When you pray for help and support as a single mother, keep this in mind: God knows what your dreams are, how far you've come, and what you most need to focus on right now in your life. God hears your sincerity and willingness to learn when you ask for guidance. He perceives the fatigue in your mind and body, your need for rest or help from others—in short, everything about you. God is in your corner 100 percent. When you run into some turbulence, make a mistake, or falter in any way, he knows what you need to do next in order to stabilize and move forward.

This book provides practical, psychological, and spiritual guidance for you as a single mother who wants the best for yourself and your family. You will always have a multitude of responsibilities, and this can be challenging, even daunting at times. Isn't it reassuring to know that you can rely on God as your advocate and guide?

> He gives power to those who are tired and worn out; he offers strength to the weak. Even youths will become exhausted, and young men will give up. But those who wait on the LORD will find new strength. They will fly high on wings like eagles. They will run and not grow weary. They will walk and not faint.
>
> Isaiah 40:29–31

1

God Loves Single Mothers

As a newlywed at age seventeen, I would get a bit upset when friends or neighbors "helpfully" remarked, "You know, teenage marriages have a 50 percent chance of ending in divorce." When I had my first child at twenty, I thought we'd beaten the odds. But a few years later I found myself, at twenty-five, starting over again. When we fall in love, get married, and have children, we don't expect or want to become divorced or widowed, and I was no exception. We go through painful times when we first become single mothers, but with determination to provide for our children and faith that God will guide us, we can turn the situation around.

I wish I'd known at age twenty-five that God loves single mothers just as much as married ones and that even after the loss and confusion of my divorce, God would still be on my side. I felt that I, along with my marriage, had failed, that I'd been immature (true), and that I deserved any and all problems that I subsequently faced (not true). What I didn't realize was that God is there for us even when we've married too young, made blunders, and found ourselves parenting solo. Though I felt at that time that God loved me in a vague, distant way, I also secretly felt that God was very disappointed in me and hence no longer supportive.

Looking back at my journal from those days, it's clear that I felt I had to do everything on my own power. I tried to be entirely independent at first. Then, with experience, I began to realize that I needed help and support from others. I ultimately came to understand that God would be there for me and that I could make a fresh start. Take a look at my early adjustments to single motherhood, and see if you can identify with any of these feelings and concerns.

1. *I feared single motherhood.* I'd never been a single mother before. How could I ever handle everything on my own while making a living and going to school? And what about all those all-nighters when a child has the flu and needs a parent's watchfulness and care? When there's only one parent, there's no such thing as tag-team relief with one's partner: "Honey, would you get the medicine while I take her to the bathroom?" or "Go back to sleep; I'll take his temperature this time." When you're a single parent, the buck stops with you.

As every single mother knows, I had to face the fact that from then on, I'd have to be the one—the only one—in charge. I'd have to start making decisions and handling crises on my own. I faced the world alone with hope and trepidation, my five-year-old daughter at my side and an application for graduate school in my hand.

I was determined to achieve my goals and didn't want divorce to get in the way. Divorce *didn't* get in the way of my education, but single motherhood was another story. I had to squeeze my research and writing work into every spare moment. I toiled such long hours at my desk that my daughter joked to her friends that all she ever saw of me was the back of my head!

Money was always short, so I had to work a couple of jobs while going to school. Some days the only thing that got me through was an old film that portrayed a poor single mother working her way through college. That video, which I rented over and over again, provided me with a positive single-mother role model of strength, perseverance, and dedication to family.

Grad school was perfect for meeting new friends. My weekly women's group met over bagels to talk about coursework and, of course, our fellow students of the male variety. It was an exciting time of learning and fun.

But there were also difficult days. It's easy to forget the lonely times or those mornings when I lay in bed thinking, "Oh no, not again!" as the alarm went off at 5:15, after I'd gotten to sleep at 2:30. It's tempting to forget those moments when I felt like a misfit because I couldn't be carefree or spontaneous like my classmates who didn't have spouses or children. If I wore rose-colored glasses, I could tell you that I never felt afraid. But that wouldn't be true.

2. *I misunderstood single motherhood.* Like many single mothers, I had "those days" when I felt that I was failing at everything: parenting, schoolwork, house cleaning, bill paying, and duties at work. I wanted to prove that I was grown up, responsible, and capable of taking care of my little family, so I tried to hide my very real needs for guidance and support—even from myself.

I didn't understand at the time what it meant to be a single mother; I mistook forced self-sufficiency for true strength. It would have been far wiser to admit that I was not, and never would be, Superwoman, than to keep the stiff upper lip I tried so hard to maintain in those days. Everyone needs a shoulder to cry on and a helping hand from time to time, not to mention the guidance of those with more experience. Unfortunately, I did without help because I worried that others would think I couldn't handle single motherhood if I revealed my normal human needs.

This feeling that we are, or need to be, totally self-sufficient is draining, stifles new learning, and can lead us to retreat into our own little self-sufficient shell. Single mothers must juggle all the balls of personal and family life, which requires a good deal of self-control and nose-to-the-grindstone effort. We can find ourselves falling into the trap of working so hard to do everything right that we go too far in this direction, subconsciously trying to prove to the world *and to God* that we are Superwomen and don't need anybody's help, thank you.

3. *I was unprepared for single motherhood.* Whatever your age, income, education, number of children, and other particulars, you probably have more in common with other single moms than you realize. We have to be all things to our children, communicate with their father (which may be easy or stressful, depending on the situation), take care of ourselves, and plan for the future—all at the same time. I don't know about you, but while I loved being a mother, I was unprepared to take on such a Herculean role.

Of course we all do our best for our children, prepared or not. When I look back at the journal I kept back in the 1980s, I can see many of the same needs that countless other single mothers have shared with me over the years. Ask yourself which of the following concerns have been relevant to you too:

- understanding and managing my emotions
- juggling my daughter's needs with my classes, work, friendships and dating
- maintaining a good child-care network, so that I could depend on responsible parents to care for my child and they could depend on me
- feeling that I deserved self-care or that this was a priority
- understanding how to manage (and stretch) money

- learning how to be considerate but assertive with authority figures such as my professors, landlords, and my child's teachers
- understanding myself, including what I really wanted and cared about, what I should do next, and how I could achieve my goals
- knowing how to best guide my daughter so she would feel loved, self-confident, and optimistic about life
- tackling my fears that God disapproved of me and learning to believe that he wanted the best for me and my family
- devising a schedule and system for cleaning to avoid either wasting precious time on housework or letting things get out of hand
- enduring the lonely times when it seemed I was missing out on all the fun because of my responsibilities as a single mother
- examining my philosophy of life and understanding where work, play, and motherhood fit in

Do any of these sound familiar? I used to think that I was unusual to have so many questions and uncertainties. Now I know that every thinking person searches for answers and guidance. Young people are trying to figure out who they are and what they're about, and older adults are trying to do the same thing.

When you're a single parent, however, the questions take on a greater urgency: you're asking not only for your own sake but for the sake of your family. If you're stuck in a confusing, depressing, or anxiety-provoking period, your children are almost sure to be affected in some way. But before you start feeling guilty, remember that you're only human, and so am I. Like anybody else, we single mothers can't avoid the hard times, but we *can* keep searching for a better way—especially when we have faith that God wants us to succeed and be happy.

The Biggest Difference between Single Mothers

Often when people talk about "single mothers," they don't seem to realize that we're not one monolithic entity. Single mothers differ from one another in attitudes, values, occupations, income, education, and priorities. While we share many of the same concerns, each of us is, in a word, unique. And one of the most fundamental differences among us is the way we think about our lives as individuals, as women, and as single moms: either we think we deserve the very best that life has to offer, or we think we'd better just "lie low" and take what we can get.

This mind-set determines what we aim for, experience, and achieve in life. It reflects how we see ourselves, what we assume that others think of us, and how we imagine God sees us. Whenever we try something new or have to make a decision, we tend to think in terms of *surviving* (just getting by from day to day) or of *thriving* (following our dreams for an abundant, joyful life).

Think about some of your past decisions or something you're grappling with now. Do you tend to aim low, spending all your time handling problems or putting out fires, or do you actively plan for and expect the best for your child and yourself? You may be wealthy or broke, getting a promotion or standing in the unemployment line, in a relationship or looking for one—whatever your current circumstances, your mind-set influences everything

The Bright Side of Single Mothering

When you make mistakes as a parent, know that you've inadvertently hurt your child's feelings, or sense that he or she feels "unheard" and misunderstood, you can quickly examine what went wrong and why. For example, were you rushed and snappy, or did you expect too much maturity of your child? You can then apologize and make amends, without having to convince a partner that your child was treated unfairly or without sufficient consideration of his or her developmental level.

you do, your aspirations, and whether you dread or look forward to the future.

To Survive or to Thrive—*That* Is the Question

Because we have to handle so many responsibilities, we often find ourselves expecting little more than getting through the next few weeks, days, or even hours. It's helpful to evaluate your attitude and your expectations because your level of optimism and hope affects both you and your children.

Ask yourself what you really feel that you deserve or can hope to achieve and what, as a consequence, you aim for: to survive or to thrive? Consider your answers to the following questions, being really honest with yourself:

1. When it comes to the future, I always plan for the worst. That way, if something good happens it will be a nice surprise, but if something bad happens I won't be disappointed.

   Totally Agree ☐   Not Sure ☐   Totally Disagree ☐

2. Single mothers have to accept that their lives will be hard. We have no partner to help us, so we have to sacrifice what we really want again and again.

   Totally Agree ☐   Not Sure ☐   Totally Disagree ☐

3. Married mothers have it easy. Single mothers are lucky just to get through the day and keep a roof over their heads.

   Totally Agree ☐   Not Sure ☐   Totally Disagree ☐

4. When my child has a problem, I know it's at least partly because I'm not married. A single mother's children are bound to have problems.

   Totally Agree ☐   Not Sure ☐   Totally Disagree ☐

5. When you're a single mother, your own happiness has to take a backseat.

   Totally Agree ☐   Not Sure ☐   Totally Disagree ☐

6. I can't expect to have a close relationship with my child the way stay-at-home married mothers can because I have to work and use child care and because I'm often tired when I'm at home.

   Totally Agree ☐   Not Sure ☐   Totally Disagree ☐

7. As a single mother, I'm naturally going to feel frazzled and over-whelmed most of the time.

   Totally Agree ☐   Not Sure ☐   Totally Disagree ☐

8. Single mothers are either irresponsible and obsessed with finding a husband or responsible and lonely.

   Totally Agree ☐   Not Sure ☐   Totally Disagree ☐

9. If you're still single after several years of single motherhood, you'll never be married and should stop trying. It's best to adjust to the fact that "your ship has sailed" and it's too late for love and marriage.

   Totally Agree ☐   Not Sure ☐   Totally Disagree ☐

10. When single mothers get tired, stressed, confused, or discour-aged, it's a sign that we've messed up.

   Totally Agree ☐   Not Sure ☐   Totally Disagree ☐

To find your score: For each "Totally Agree" or "Not Sure" an-swer, give yourself one point. For each "Totally Disagree," give yourself ten points. Now add all the points from all ten questions to get your final score.

This little quiz isn't a psychological test, but it is designed to help you become more aware of your assumptions. Your score will help you gain insight regarding which of three categories your current approach to single mothering falls into: Just Surviving, Unsure, or Thriving. You may see a bit of yourself in two categories or in all three. Or you may see yourself in one category most of the time and in another only when you're feeling tired or stressed out or you have a bad head cold. Whatever the pattern, it can be helpful to discover beliefs or attitudes that you didn't realize you had, mistaken ideas that have been deposited over the years by individuals in your life or by media stereotypes.

You may also recognize some important strengths or little victories over self-doubt that you've won along the way. Find a quiet time and place to explore your true feelings about yourself, your family, and your relationship with God. You may also want to write in a journal to record the feelings, memories, or realizations that come to you as you go through this exercise.

Are You Just Surviving or Thriving?

10–30 Points: Just Surviving. Somewhere along the line, you've bought into the myth that single mothers and their families can't be as fortunate or happy as married parents and their families. You may have lost faith in yourself or in your child's potential. Sometimes you wonder if God watches over single mothers, or you in particular, at all.

If this is you, don't despair. The good news is, you're going to be learning about yourself, realizing how you've passed through (or may still feel stuck in) challenging or difficult situations, and how you may have been holding yourself back with negative self-talk. You'll also learn how to recognize the signs that you're getting overtired, overwhelmed, or discouraged and when you need to strengthen your self-care and your faith. Resolve right now to remodel these faulty attitudes and assumptions as you work your way through this book.

40–70 Points: Unsure. You're a bit more optimistic about single motherhood in general and your life in particular than are the Just Surviving moms. You've adjusted fairly well to life as a single mother and haven't given up on all your dreams. But you're unsure about "going for the gusto" and often feel insecure.

Sometimes you think you've made too many mistakes or have waited too long to aim for what would make you and your family happiest. While you recognize that God loves single mothers and wants to support and guide you, sometimes when you hear references to "broken homes" or "fatherless homes," you wonder if your children can grow up to be well-adjusted with "just you" at the helm.

If you recognize this pattern of sometimes-optimism and sometimes-pessimism here, take heart: you don't yet have the positive mind-set you need, but by being honest with yourself, you're on your way to a better life—not only for you but for your children too. Read this book with an eye to casting out every doubt, rooting out every fear that you don't deserve the best, and shoring up your faith and confidence.

80–100 Points: Thriving. You value yourself and shoot for the stars, convinced that single mothers can and should aim as high as anyone else. You understand that every family is different, whether headed by a couple or a single parent. As such, you expect no less for your children than for those with married parents.

When you run up against limitations or obstacles, you see them for what they are: challenges to be overcome or worked around. You feel confident that God is on your side and is always there to support and guide you. While you may sometimes feel overwhelmed by daily demands, you understand that married parents get overwhelmed too! In other words, you don't chalk up all your problems or your child's problems to single motherhood. You're both optimistic and realistic—a healthy combination.

If this is you, congratulations! You've avoided the pitfalls of self-doubt that snare many single mothers. As a Thriving single mother, you can return to this book time and again, whenever you need a little boost as you follow your dreams.

Take my yoke upon you and learn from me.

Matthew 11:29 NIV

Anyone who listens to my teaching and obeys me is wise, like a person who builds a house on solid rock.

Matthew 7:24

She deploys her strength from one end of the earth to the other, ordering all things for good.

Wisdom 8:1 JB

Lord, please help me to build my house on the solid rock of your teachings. Whenever I feel overtired or needy, remind me to stop and pray so that I can learn from you, increase my understanding, and feel supported and confident once again. Amen.

2

The Single Mother's Inventory

How are you and your children doing? Sometimes it's difficult to know for sure while you're in the thick of things. As a busy single mom, you may find yourself attending to only the latest needs or problems. Less urgent matters, some of which may warrant your attention, can slip past your radar. The Single Mother's Inventory can help you step back and evaluate the many areas of your child's life and your own. The questions below are designed to help you determine what's going well and what areas could use improvement. Find a peaceful time and place to rate the status of each area from 1 to 4, as objectively as possible. If you know of special circumstances influencing a situation, make a note of this next to each item.

If you notice that some answers are not what you would have hoped, keep in mind that the purpose of this inventory is to help you get a wide-angle view of your life and your child's life. Most importantly, the ultimate goal of answering these questions is to acknowledge and feel good about the strong points and to observe the areas that need improvement or repair.

You may find that you want to build on the areas that are already going well. This is a great idea and wise as well: you'll become more resilient when you regularly focus on the bright spots in your life and allow yourself to feel good about your goals, achievements, and blessings.

Two notes before you begin:

1. For all questions, respond according to the last couple of months. That time period usually captures what's generally going on in a person's life without the distortion of "used-to-bes" and "hope-to-soons."

The only exception has to do with those items regarding your child's school-related issues (school work, grades, friends, relationships with teachers, etc.). If you're answering this during summer break or at the beginning of a new school year, refer to the last two months of school. Life changes quickly, and this inventory is designed to help you get a current, valid snapshot of how things are going for you and your children.

2. When answering the questions about your child, answer separately for each child. I know this adds to the task, but it's vitally important to get an accurate picture regarding each individual. It may help to make copies of the inventory before filling it out or to attach a separate answer sheet for each child.

In some cases we tend to evaluate our children as a group because we don't immediately notice subtle differences. In other cases, we tend to answer for the child with whom we feel the most rapport and who's doing best in school, or we think of our "problem child." By answering questions separately for each child, you'll gain a lot of clarity.

Give each item careful thought and circle the rating that's most accurate. Again, use this inventory to spark your awareness of these and any other issues that may come to mind, making notes in the margins or circling those questions that are especially important to you.

All about You

Your Psychological and Emotional Health

1. How emotionally balanced and psychologically healthy do you feel?

1	2	3	4
Not at all	Needs some improvement	Better than in the past	Doing very well

2. How well are you able, in general, to concentrate, focus on tasks, solve problems, and remember important information?

1	2	3	4
Not at all	Needs some improvement	Better than in the past	Doing very well

Your Physical Health and Energy Level

3. How well are you eating healthy foods, getting regular medical checkups, and generally taking care of your health and physical fitness?

1	2	3	4
Not at all	Needs some improvement	Better than in the past	Doing very well

4. How free do you feel from addictions to alcohol, drugs, sex, compulsive work, overeating/binging/purging, or watching too much television or other media?

1	2	3	4
Not at all	Needs some improvement	Better than in the past	Doing very well

Your Child Care Support Network

5. How adequate and reliable is your child care situation covering your work hours?

1	2	3	4
Not at all	Needs some improvement	Better than in the past	Doing very well

6. How adequate and reliable is your support network for the purpose of giving you regular "time off" and allowing you to handle emergencies? (To rate "4," your network should consist of at least two reliable people.)

1	2	3	4
Not at all	Needs some improvement	Better than in the past	Doing very well

Your Relationship with Your Child

7. How stress-free and enjoyable (to you) is your relationship with your child?

1	2	3	4
Not at all	Needs some improvement	Better than in the past	Doing very well

8. To what degree do you feel similar to and/or that you're "on the same wavelength" with your child?

1	2	3	4
Not at all	Needs some improvement	Better than in the past	Doing very well

Your Relationship with Your Child's Father

9. How calmly and effectively do you and your child's father communicate, plan cooperatively, and share at least some responsibilities regarding your child?

1	2	3	4
Not at all	Needs some improvement	Better than in the past	Doing very well

10. How reliable is your child's father when it comes to paying child support on time and in the amount agreed upon, arriving on time for visitation or joint custody transfers, etc.?

1	2	3	4
Not at all	Needs some improvement	Better than in the past	Doing very well

Your Relationships with Others

11. How healthy and satisfying are your relationships with most of the people in your life?

1	2	3	4
Not at all	Needs some improvement	Better than in the past	Doing very well

12. How content do you feel at this time in your life (as opposed to feeling abandoned, or lonely and wishing for a boyfriend or husband)?

1	2	3	4
Not at all	Needs some improvement	Better than in the past	Doing very well

Organization: Household and Paperwork

13. How quickly and easily can you find essential papers and written records (birth certificates, bank statements, home leases or mortgage papers, automobile records, insurance policies, tax returns, addresses of essential contacts, etc.)?

1	2	3	4
Not at all	Needs some improvement	Better than in the past	Doing very well

14. How quickly and easily can you find things such as your car keys, your sunglasses, your child's gloves, your un-ripped pantyhose, your to-do list or appointment book, your child's flip-flops, or the lid that goes with the saucepan you rarely use?

1	2	3	4
Not at all	Needs some improvement	Better than in the past	Doing very well

Your Financial Situation

15. How secure do you feel about the amount of money available to you each month for the basics: shelter, food, paying bills, clothing, school supplies, etc.?

1	2	3	4
Not at all	Needs some improvement	Better than in the past	Doing very well

16. To what degree does your current income allow you to get out from under debt and/or to get ahead financially so that you have extra funds to draw on when unexpected costs (car, home repairs, children's school fees or uniforms, dental visits, etc.) must be paid?

1	2	3	4
Not at all	Needs some improvement	Better than in the past	Doing very well

Your Job and Career

17. To what degree is your job meeting *your basic needs*: (a) health (contributing to your/your children's health or at least not causing physical risk or harm to you or your children) and (b) safety (providing at least adequate income to pay the bills, keep a roof over your heads and food on the table, etc.)?

1	2	3	4
Not at all	Needs some improvement	Better than in the past	Doing very well

18. To what degree is your job meeting *your higher needs*: (a) camaraderie, social interaction, a sense of teamwork/belonging, (b) self-esteem, knowing that you're doing good work and providing for your family, and (c) self-actualization, feeling that your talents are being put to good use; a sense of meaning and purpose?

1	2	3	4
Not at all	Needs some improvement	Better than in the past	Doing very well

Your Interests, Hobbies, and Dreams

19. How well do you currently devote time to those things you truly love—painting, going to places you enjoy, swimming, sewing, writing, gardening, traveling, camping, etc.?

1	2	3	4
Not at all	Needs some improvement	Better than in the past	Doing very well

20. If you stay in your current situation in terms of work, income, co-workers, friends, living arrangement, etc., to what degree do you think you can begin or reenter those interests, hobbies, or big dream activities that you long to immerse yourself in for the pure joy of it?

1	2	3	4
Not at all	Needs some improvement	Better than in the past	Doing very well

Your Spiritual Life

21. How confident do you feel that God is on your side 100 percent?

1	2	3	4
Not at all	Needs some improvement	Better than in the past	Doing very well

22. How easy is it for you to ask God for what you need in prayer and for you to feel nourished, more clear about a situation, or more at peace when God answers?

1	2	3	4
Not at all	Needs some improvement	Better than in the past	Doing very well

All about Your Child

(Remember to answer this section separately for each child)

Your Child's Psychological and Emotional Health

23. How generally happy (as opposed to having low self-esteem or frequently feeling sad, anxious, angry, noncommunicative, or lonely) does your child appear to be?

1	2	3	4
Not at all	Needs some improvement	Better than in the past	Doing very well

24. When you set limits, or consequences for violating limits, how well can your child usually accept those limits or consequences (that is, without having huge tantrums, arguing endlessly, slamming doors, or reacting just the opposite—anxious or fearful obedience and compliance, isolating in his or her bedroom, or appearing very sad or passive with an "I give up" facial expression)?

1	2	3	4
Not at all	Needs some improvement	Better than in the past	Doing very well

Your Child's Physical Health

25. To what degree is your child doing well in terms of health, fitness, and energy level?

1	2	3	4
Not at all	Needs some improvement	Better than in the past	Doing very well

26. To what degree is your child doing well with regard to his or her past medical problems (for example, chronic allergies, asthma, being overweight, or frequent [known or suspected] smoking/alcohol/drug use)?

1	2	3	4
Not at all	Needs some improvement	Better than in the past	Doing very well

Your Child's Academic Functioning

27. How well is your child doing in school and in doing homework (consider grades here, not just whether or not a given teacher and your child get along)?

1	2	3	4
Not at all	Needs some improvement	Better than in the past	Doing very well

28. How effective is your child's concentration and ability to focus on schoolwork (both at school and in a homework setting) without getting overly distracted or hyperactive?

1	2	3	4
Not at all	Needs some improvement	Better than in the past	Doing very well

Your Child's Relationship with You

29. How much does your child open up to you and communicate clearly without worrying that you're too busy or distracted to really hear him or her, that you'll fall apart emotionally (cry, feel rejected, etc.), or that lying is necessary to avoid punishment or avoid making you angry or "setting you off"?

1	2	3	4
Not at all	Needs some improvement	Better than in the past	Doing very well

30. To what degree does your child see you as an advocate, a trusted guide, and an emotional supporter rather than a nagger, complainer, or mostly a disciplinarian?

1	2	3	4
Not at all	Needs some improvement	Better than in the past	Doing very well

Your Child's Relationship with His or Her Father

31. How emotionally close does your child feel to his or her dad (if he's involved)?

1	2	3	4
Not at all	Needs some improvement	Better than in the past	Doing very well

32. How reliable is your child's father in terms of showing up when planned, maintaining a stable mood and refraining from substance abuse when with him or her, and communicating with you in an adequately respectful way in front of the child?

1	2	3	4
Not at all	Needs some improvement	Better than in the past	Doing very well

Your Child's Relationships with Others

33. How effective and polished are your child's social skills—that is, ability to make good eye contact, make friends (even if just a few good friends), show empathy, inhibit impulsive remarks that could create conflicts or hurt feelings, share toys (even if he or she needs to be reminded now and then), listen to others, and be generally respectful and polite?

1	2	3	4
Not at all	Needs some improvement	Better than in the past	Doing very well

34. How confident (as opposed to discouraged or socially anxious) does your child feel about his or her ability to make and keep friends and interact well with peers at school, in the neighborhood, and in other situations?

1	2	3	4
Not at all	Needs some improvement	Better than in the past	Doing very well

Your Child's Ability to Manage Chores and Homework

35. To what degree does your child have a reasonable number of household chores assigned to him or her that are appropriate to age, developmental/maturity level, time available after schoolwork demands, and his or her unique set of initiation/implementation skills?

1	2	3	4
Not at all	Needs some improvement	Better than in the past	Doing very well

36. How well is your child's desk or other homework "command central" station organized so that it's as easy, comfortable, and appealing as possible to gather needed materials, sit down, and get busy with good lighting and perhaps a fun or inspirational poster?

1	2	3	4
Not at all	Needs some improvement	Better than in the past	Doing very well

Child's Interests, Play, and Downtime

37. How many opportunities per week does your child usually have to engage in his or her interests, unstructured play, spirit-renewing downtime, or having lots of fun?

1	2	3	4
Not at all	Needs some improvement	Better than in the past	Doing very well

38. To what degree do you already know what your child most loves doing?

1	2	3	4
Not at all	Needs some improvement	Better than in the past	Doing very well

Your Child's Dreams and Goals

39. How often does your child talk about dreams and goals—that is, what he or she wants to try, learn about, accomplish, or devote his or her life to someday?

1	2	3	4
Not at all	Needs some improvement	Better than in the past	Doing very well

40. How vigorously do you encourage your child's right to dream big, even when you know those dreams may change over time or that your child will have to work very hard, develop more persistence/focus, or find alternate routes to pursue those interests?

1	2	3	4
Not at all	Needs some improvement	Better than in the past	Doing very well

Your Child's Spiritual Development

41. To what degree does your child feel confident that God is loving, is not punitive, and is interested in every aspect of his or her life?

1	2	3	4
Not at all	Needs some improvement	Better than in the past	Doing very well

42. How would you describe your child's understanding of the important values that Jesus taught, such as empathy for others, kindness, helping the less fortunate, and feeling free to pray for oneself and for others?

1	2	3	4
Not at all	Needs some improvement	Better than in the past	Doing very well

How to Interpret Your Results

This is a qualitative inventory, not a scientific test, so interpreting your scores is something that you can do in an intuitive way. Clearly, the more 3s and 4s you marked, the better you're probably feeling about your life and your children's lives. Having a lot of 2s indicates that you want to make improvements but doesn't suggest that a crisis situation exists. The more 1s you marked, of course, the more concerned you are about the way things are going in that part of your life or your child's life, and the more likely you feel that a crisis already exists or is brewing.

What may be most helpful is to note:

1. any answers that surprised you, which may represent areas that you may not have given much thought to recently;
2. any *patterns* of 3s and 4s or of 1s and 2s that cause you to notice where you may have been staying on top of things or feeling satisfied, versus areas of life that you've been failing to notice or have been letting go for too long;
3. important realizations and insights that you discovered through notes that you made next to certain items;
4. more than ten responses at the "Not at all" level (1) suggests that you're feeling at least somewhat overwhelmed. If you have marked more than twenty answers at the "1" level, you may feel that you're in crisis mode, or at the very least that you're spending far too much time "putting out fires" rather

than making good progress, enjoying your life, and feeling strong faith and confidence.

You now have a more comprehensive perspective of how well things are going for you and your child on a daily basis—though of course this is a very incomplete list of the single mother's concerns, needs, and responsibilities. Be sure to celebrate your efforts for those areas that you rated as 3s and 4s. Take a moment to pray for guidance in making improvements to the areas that you rated as 2s and 3s. Ask for extra strength and wisdom to tackle the 1s. Finally, examine any notes you've made throughout this process, and feel good about giving your family all of this loving, careful time and attention.

> Therefore I tell you, whatever you ask for in prayer, believe that you have received it, and it will be yours.
>
> Mark 11:24 NIV
>
> Intelligent people are always open to new ideas. In fact, they look for them.
>
> Proverbs 18:15

3

Single Mother, CEO

You are the head of a very important organization. Your decisions regarding the long-term mission and direction of this company influence the lives of those under your command, people whose present and future lives depend not only on those decisions but on your short-term goals, directives, and especially actions. Sometimes your people look up to you. Sometimes they wait for your instructions. Sometimes they resent you. Sometimes they threaten to go on strike! But they always need you. Without your leadership, they would be adrift, and the whole organization would collapse due to inefficiency and chaos.

"They," of course, are your children, and you are the CEO. Like it or not, you as a single mother are at the helm. The organization rises and falls based on your ability to understand what needs to be done now, what needs doing in the future, and how to make corrections and improvements whenever new needs or challenges arise.

Danielle was trying to make the right decisions for herself and for her children, especially with regards to money, housing, and schooling. However, she often ended up second-guessing herself, wondering if her plans made sense at all. Danielle was frequently concerned about making the right decisions: "I do miss that part of being married. I'm never quite sure I've done the right thing. This is what I really, really envy about married parents—they have someone to bounce ideas off of, somebody to look at the pros and cons with them—and then they make goals and decisions *together*. If whatever they decided doesn't work out, there's no one person to blame; also, they can then get busy finding a better solution *together*, and you know what they say: two heads are better than one."

Danielle noted that she's a working mother who looks to outsiders as if she knows what she's doing, yet at least half the time she feels like a child herself, wishing she had a partner to help her figure out what to do next. Danielle was tired of always worrying about making the best decision, and of just avoiding making a decision at all.

Two misconceptions in what Danielle expressed needed to be cleared up. First, a lot of those married couples we assume to be in such great harmony and communication *aren't*. In fact, one of the most frequent complaints I hear from married parents (usually mothers, for whatever reason) is that they end up making all the decisions or holding the bag when things go wrong.

Another complaint, perhaps even more widespread, is that husband and wife simply disagree at fundamental levels regarding the best approach to raising their children, deciding where to live, managing financial problems, juggling two careers and child care equitably, and so on. When this is the case, all the brainstorming in the world isn't going to lead to a good decision, or any decision at all. What it may lead to, in fact, is a very angry slamming of doors or the silent treatment. Thus one parent ends up making all the decisions, just as you're doing, but must also face arguments, resentment, or undermining on a regular basis. I

> **The Bright Side of Single Mothering**
>
> You can design and create a home atmosphere to your liking, and you can creatively influence your child's environment with independent decision making.

know you're longing for a great partner, but for now, count your single-mother blessings!

The second misconception applies to everyone on earth: that is, if leadership skills; smart, strategic planning; or wisdom don't come naturally by the time a person reaches adulthood, they're out of reach, the secret "gifts" of successful people. Nobody is born with leadership skills; these abilities must be learned. If you were one of the few whose parents taught or modeled exceptional leadership skills or made sure you were involved in some form of leadership development activities, this learning may have come more easily and naturally. For most people, this wasn't the case. We need to accept the fact that in order to become good leaders for our families, we may need to start from scratch.

You've already recognized your tendency to delay or second-guess your decisions and that you often feel like a child inside who simply doesn't know *how* to make good decisions, set reasonable goals, and then carry them out. This is an area in which you realize you need to improve, which is a step in the right direction. There are many ways to develop your leadership skills, including your long-range perspective and your confidence (self-doubt is destructive when it becomes a habit), and you'll find references in the back of this book to help you do so.

But if you're facing some kind of crisis or otherwise urgent situation, I'd advise you to supplement your long-term learning and development by consulting with people who already have the kinds of savvy and information necessary in order to make the best decisions. This could be an "older, wiser" person from your social or family circle or a professional advisor or therapist. Don't seek guidance from someone who can offer sympathy or commiseration but whose own life doesn't provide evidence that he or she really knows more than you do about the issues you're facing.

The CEO in You

You may not feel like a CEO right now. You may wonder, in fact, how on earth you got this job. You may not have the foggiest idea what a CEO does, let alone how she does it—but you're about to learn, and both you and your children will benefit from your development as a leader. Fortunately for you, there are many great resources out there to help you learn the ropes of your executive and managerial roles. For now, let's go over a few basics that I've found particularly helpful, both for myself and for my clients.

Long-Term vs. Short-Term Objectives

As your family's CEO, you'll eventually need to allow yourself time to get in touch with your dreams for the future and to articulate what it is you most want for you and your child. However, contrary to what many people assume, it's best *not* to start by spending too much time on the big picture if there are pressing problems or short-term challenges that you need to resolve. While allowing yourself to dream big will certainly be in order soon, doing so

---

The Bright Side of Single Mothering

Your child is likely to develop capacities for responsibility and independence because he or she recognizes that you are a single parent. (Note: This will at times seem highly doubtful, judging by his or her apparent obliviousness to your limitations! However, in general you'll notice this trend toward self-sufficiency as your child gets older.)

while you're in the thick of things and need to learn new leadership skills isn't where your time is best spent. Over time you'll develop and fine-tune your values, goals, and visions for yourself and your family—but the first order of business is to evaluate where you and your family are at this time and which problems need to be brought under control.

If you completed the inventory in chapter 2, you probably know, or are developing greater clarity regarding, the areas that most need improvement. If the need for change feels daunting to consider, just relax: all you need is the commitment to gain control over those areas and a good game plan for getting started.

I offer the following ten steps to self and family improvement that are highly effective. I hope you'll use them with confidence, just as you would a tried-and-true recipe that won't fail as long as you include the specified ingredients and follow, as closely as you can, the steps in the order given.

I discovered this ten-step strategy over much time and after great trouble, much effort, missteps, wrong turns, and actively learning from everyone I could find—authors, professionals, friends, family members, even strangers. Try it! Each time you do, you'll notice that the process comes more naturally to you and that your leadership capacity is enhanced.

10 Steps to Family and Self Improvement

1. Before beginning any changes, arrange some "alone time" during which you can relax and think clearly. You need to have sufficient time to sit quietly without noise, demands, or distractions. To make the shift from reacting or putting out fires to proactive leadership, you'll need to get out of busy or crisis mode in order to achieve the mental clarity and gather sufficient information to respond and plan wisely. As your family's CEO you must, like any CEO, arrange for

regularly available blocks of time in which to quietly reflect, troubleshoot, and evaluate your resources. Resources may include people who can help, advise, or encourage you; money; supplies; your knowledge, skills, and talents; and so on.

2. Review your responses to the Single Mother's Inventory to refresh yourself on what's working and what isn't. Be thorough. Honestly evaluate each domain, including any issues or problems that weren't included, until you feel confident that you've covered every important area of your life and your child's life. List them all without an ounce of judgment or guilt. If you get anxious at any point, remind yourself that everything's going to be okay, because now you're asking God to help you to become proactive, not just reactive, and to understand where you and your child are and where you want to be. In other words, you're becoming a successful CEO for your family and yourself.

3. Next, ask yourself which of those areas you listed you can handle on your own, given sufficient time, effort, and resources. If you learn over time that you were mistaken about any of these areas, you can always reassess and decide what kind of help you may need from books, professionals, friends, or other sources.

4. Now make a separate list of those challenges, unmet goals, or problems that you're not sure you know how to meet, achieve, or resolve without outside help, resources, or additional information.

5. Place these lists where you'll see them frequently: on pages in your appointment book that you tag for frequent review with a sticky note or paper clip; taped to your mirror; or in two file folders (different colors are best) that catch the eye. Whatever you do, don't file these away or allow anything to cover them. This is your life we're talking about. Keep these

lists of areas you'd like to improve front and center; don't let them get lost and forgotten under a stack of bills.

Note: You may wish to do the following steps now or when you next have some free time. If you're ready to continue, by all means do, but remember: it's better to do a little at a time if that's all you currently have the time or energy for. You're in charge, and you get to decide how much you can comfortably handle at a time.

6. Next to each item in both lists, write down in as much detail as possible what you want to achieve, that is, what success or wonderful improvement would look and feel like. Don't be overly perfectionistic (for example, if your child is barely making Ds now, it's unwise to set the goal of straight As by her next grading period), but don't be too small in your visions, either (for example, don't settle for "avoid late fees due to forgetting to pay bills on time" when you really long to "develop and maintain a financial system that prevents costly errors and increases my savings cushion for greater security and freedom").

7. Beside each item in the first list, the one you feel that you can handle without help, write down anything that would make the process of learning, problem solving, and goal achievement easier or more fun for you. Next to each item in the second list of issues, specify the kind of help you think you'll need: reading a book on the subject, asking someone for advice, or seeking the expert guidance of a professional.

8. In your appointment book or on your calendar, record a time to (a) take the next action step needed or (b) think further about what will be required to move forward on more complex items. Except for those items that are simple and quick to do (for example, "Call for appointment with vet to get the cat spayed"), try not to schedule tackling two or more important issues for the same morning or afternoon. Once

you get into the swing of this process, you can bite off more at a time; for now, just "nibble" and conserve your energy.

9. Beside the type of learning or outside assistance needed for items listed in the second list, record for any item you already know this information about: the place where you'll find the source (a certain bookstore, library, website, etc.) and/or the person you can call (with the phone number, if you have it).

10. Now it's time to set up a schedule to begin reviewing your lists on a weekly basis to determine next action steps and try to do at least one per day. If you review your lists regularly (I'd advise weekly or, better yet, twice weekly), you'll be amazed at how the most vexing, stubborn problems begin to bend to your insistent attention and little actions.

As Chris Gardner writes in *Start Where You Are*,

With action comes traction and before you know it, you're empowered to take on the more daunting challenges. Just that one decision to do something, anything, can be your antidote to feeling outgunned, especially when the deck seems stacked against you, when you're feeling like bad luck and trouble are your only friends. You will probably feel empowered five minutes into the process. Then again, it's your choice.[1]

What this boils down to is this: don't put pressure on yourself to do too much too quickly, but do begin to take baby steps toward learning leadership skills and accomplishing your goals. Even a little progress will lift your spirits.

You may feel that it's taking too long; for a time you may not see any progress, but don't get discouraged: we all have to start somewhere, and even the tiniest steps, if taken regularly, will begin to add up, such that one day you'll turn around and say to yourself, "Wow, things *have* gotten better!"

Give yourself a pat on the back, and pray for the spirit and determination to keep pressing forward whenever you feel tired, get distracted by new twists in the road, or otherwise have temporarily lost your momentum. Just "get back on the horse" as soon as you can, and keep up the good work. That's what great leadership is all about: steadily creating positive changes, one step at a time, to create a happier present and a better future.

So I say to you: Ask and it will be given to you; seek and you will find; knock and the door will be opened to you. For everyone who asks receives; he who seeks finds; and to him who knocks, the door will be opened.

Luke 11:9–10 NIV

Fools think they need no advice, but the wise listen to others.

Proverbs 12:15

So take a new grip with your tired hands and stand firm on your shaky legs. Mark out a straight path for your feet. Then those who follow you, though they are weak and lame, will not stumble and fall but will become strong.

Hebrews 12:12–13

Lord, I know being a single mother requires discernment, sensitivity, and wise decision making. I will rely on your guidance as I develop my leadership and mothering skills, and I pray for the confidence I need to become the kind of CEO that my family needs. Amen.

4

Self-Care for Single Moms

This book isn't solely about your children. While you want the very best for them, keep in mind that their happiness depends on yours. By "happiness" I don't mean that everything in your life is perfect or that you're completely satisfied or serene—I mean simply that you feel good about yourself and that you know you're committed to learning and improving: in short, that there's hope.

Happiness also comes from knowing that you truly love, forgive, and take good care of yourself. It's knowing that when you do get discouraged or disappointed because of mistakes, weaknesses, or unforeseen circumstances, you can adapt to changes, make corrections, or chart an entirely new course.

Single Mothers Often Expect Too Much of Themselves

Feeling like many single mothers, thirty-five-year-old Hannah said, "I'm trying to be the best mother I can be, but sometimes I find myself getting too worked up over little problems or too worried to do what I need to do about the big ones. I don't know what's wrong with me—why can't I just be happy?"

That last sentence was a giveaway to at least part of the problem, and Hannah agreed that this was her primary impediment: self-criticism and self-blame. Hannah berated herself frequently for not "just being happy," but this was simply an example of the negative self-talk that had long ago become a habit. In fact, Hannah had come to accept the negative statements she frequently said to herself as "realistic." Deep down, she was expecting herself to deal with all the demands of work and single motherhood with the same degree of ease and fun that her married-parent and non-parent friends seemed able to experience.

Hannah was expecting far too much of herself, which of course led to disappointment and frustration with herself. Single moms must be careful to avoid comparing themselves to those who carry fewer or shared responsibilities as parents.

We can all be happy, but for many of us this goal requires inner work, shifts in attitude, and external changes for the better. When you're multitasking and juggling many responsibilities, it's natural to become anxious at times about keeping up with everything. When the anxiety is greater than the minimal amount needed to motivate us into action, however, it's counterproductive. This level of anxiety usually indicates a problem with self-esteem, a tendency to doubt oneself, and a deficit in self-care behind the scenes.

Many single mothers find they're so busy that there's little time left over for calm reflection and spiritual renewal. Doing regular emotional-physical-spiritual "check-ins" to evaluate how you're feeling and what you really need right now is essential. If you're not accustomed to doing this, try rating each of those three dimensions on a scale of 1 (lowest) to 10 (highest). Your children's needs may have been met today, but what about yours? Are you letting yourself go or failing to advocate for yourself in some way?

Additionally, when you hear yourself saying things to others or to yourself such as "What's wrong with me?" or "Why can't I just be happy?" that's your cue that you're pushing yourself too hard or expecting too much of yourself. Negative self-talk is a sign that you need to slow down and become more aware of your internal self-talk. Make a commitment to self-care that includes good physical habits (nutrition, sleep, exercise, and medical checkups) and good psychological habits, particularly relating to your inner dialogue—the things you say to yourself on a regular basis. If you've been putting everybody else first, or if you tend to cycle between self-indulgence and self-denial, learning good ongoing self-care will take some time and effort. But this is one area that will really pay off in terms of better health, more patience with the kids, and greater resilience in all areas of your life.

Caring for You

As soon as you can get a few minutes of peace and quiet—even if the only time you can find is after everyone else is asleep or before they wake up—relax, make a cup of tea or coffee or hot chocolate, and devote yourself to thinking about your needs, including those of the little girl in you.

Look around you right now. What do you see? The ideal view before you is one of beauty and order. Whether your clothes and furniture are from boutiques or thrift stores, your surroundings are pleasing to the eye so that being at home is calming and inspiring. Things are at least reasonably organized, and you see some little treasures—a piece of art, a lovely plant, or your favorite books. When you look in the mirror, you see that you've been taking good care of yourself with all the resources at your disposal. When you need support, there are caring people you can call. You may have lots of duties to attend to as a single mom, but you don't feel burdened. You regularly experience a sense of joy, fulfillment, and hope for the future. If this is your current reality, what a blessing—your inner child feels safe, secure, and cared for.

If, on the other hand, things aren't going this well—and rarely is everything going well at any given time—take heart because this is often the case for busy single moms. In fact, a somewhat neglected inner child isn't at all unusual when you're the family CEO. Even if your children help out around the house, the fact remains that you don't have a staff to carry out your plans or take care of the details. You'll find some tips in chapter 6, "Getting Organized," for taking control of clutter and making your home environment more pleasing and nurturing for you; in chapter 5, "Getting the Support You Need," you'll find ideas for developing a network to make being a single mom easier and more enjoyable.

In the meantime, let's consider some signs of inadequate self-care. What's it like when the little girl inside is feeling insecure and neglected? Here are some clues:

- You make sure your child has the best of everything, but when it comes to you, well, that can wait.
- You're focused on your child's success at school so that he can pursue his dreams someday, but you can't even remember what you once dreamed of doing.
- On a practical but important level, you insist that your child put the toys away, but your own bedroom is a disaster area—there's not enough time or energy for that, and anyway, who cares?
- You've gotten so out of shape that you can't wear any of your good clothes, and your health, energy level, and confidence are suffering as a result.
- While you may indulge in buying or doing nice things for yourself from time to time, you feel guilty and berate yourself when you do so.

- You take your child for regular medical and dental checkups, but you take yourself to the doctor or dentist only if and when painful or worrisome symptoms have reached a crisis level.

If these sound familiar, you need to ramp up your self-care. There are many small but rewarding things you can do to nurture yourself. Here are just a few examples:

- Take the time to reorganize your closet so that getting dressed in the morning is an easy, pleasant experience.
- Indulge in your favorite foods or beverages. (If you're dieting, this can be motivating as an occasional reward for sticking to good nutrition for a given period of time.)
- Read a good book or write in your journal in a pleasant coffee shop.
- Watch your favorite video, especially if it warms your heart, inspires you, or makes you laugh. Laughing in particular is a natural antidepressant: it triggers the production of endorphins, the "happy" chemicals in your brain. Plus, it's fun!
- Give yourself a manicure and pedicure, play with makeup, or try out a new hairstyle to experiment with a new image. Such "girly stuff" can be quite relaxing and helps you to refresh your "look" for work or play.
- Call a friend to talk or schedule a get-together when you need to talk to another adult. Shopping can boost your spirits (carefully select the stores that are truly relaxing and fun for you), even if you only window shop, then enjoy lunch at your favorite restaurant.
- Taking your child along with you can also be a boost when you do something child-friendly, such as going to a park on a sunny day or to a museum or matinee to cheer you both up on a stormy afternoon.

You're the expert on what will boost your spirits and help the little girl inside you feel that she's important and deserves the best of care. Treat yourself whenever you can, knowing that your parenting abilities are at their best when your inner self feels as valued and loved as your own children do.

Good Inner Dialogue Is Good Self-Care

What do you say when you talk to yourself? A pivotal part of self-care includes monitoring your inner dialogue and, when necessary, making changes so that you're inwardly supporting yourself and encouraging an optimistic perspective when challenging situations pop up in your life. Becoming aware of your self-talk is essential because:

1. you already talk to yourself, whether you realize it or not: depending on what you say and hear in your mind day in and day out, it's either helping you or hurting you; and
2. your success in every area in your life—including parenting— depends heavily on whether that inner dialogue is generally negative or positive in tone.

Some people talk to themselves silently, in their minds. Others may talk to themselves out loud when they're alone and are sure nobody will hear them. Most of us talk to ourselves aloud even when we're not alone, "under our breath," while trying to remember something (for example, "I just *know* I left my wallet right here—where can it be?"). This is simply an audible form of our continuously streaming mental thoughts. Likewise, we may whisper to ourselves reminders of things we need to do, such as, "Okay, don't forget, pick Sarah up at 2:15 today for her dental appointment," or saying as we look in the mirror for an important meeting, "Remember now, stay calm."

The Bright Side of Single Mothering

In many cases, you can be happier because there's nobody to "bring you down" with pessimism or negativity. This can be a huge gift to you as well as your child if your husband tended toward irritability, pessimism, or grumpiness. As the "mood leader" in your family, you can set a positive, upbeat tone for your children. They will likely, as a result, gradually become more positive and optimistic themselves if you've been modeling a realistic yet hopeful perspective.

We may also, unless we become aware of this and intentionally change it, talk to ourselves in a negative way. When we're tired or stressed—familiar states for mothers—this type of self-talk can really take a toll. Even the most confident person with the highest self-esteem has at some time or another whispered under her breath, "Oh, you idiot! How could you have forgotten *that?*" or "I was so irritable tonight, what a terrible mother I am," or "Nothing's ever going to get better for me; I give up."

Why is it so vital that you monitor and improve your self-talk? Because the wrong words said to yourself, especially if you "hear" them on a regular basis, don't just hurt you—they're bound to impact your children as well because they depend so much on you. Our children readily "soak up" our habitual ways of thinking and feeling, our attitudes, and our confidence. Needless to say, this can be either a good thing or a bad thing, depending on our mental habits and inner dialogue.

A 30-Day Plan to Trade Negative Self-Talk for Positive Inner Dialogue

Maybe changing anxious or self-critical thinking isn't a struggle for you. If so, you probably grew up hearing words of praise rather than criticism and hope versus discouragement, and thus you naturally developed your own optimistic and encouraging self-talk.

**Childhood Experiences Can Influence Your Self-Talk—
But You Can Change All That**

Don't say about yourself what others say unless what they say is worth
repeating. Perhaps your parents spoke to you in a way that caused you
to lack confidence. They may not have known any better, but the good
news is, you don't have to be affected by their words for the rest of your
life. You can change your image of yourself beginning right now!

Joyce Meyer, *The Confident Woman*[1]

But if you're like most people, you'll have to change your inner
dialogue in small and large ways. You may need to replace those
easily-discouraged or self-blaming habitual thoughts with more
reasonable, supportive, and uplifting inner dialogue.

1. During week one, don't try to change anything; just "listen."
Become aware of what you say to yourself throughout the day,
whether silently or out loud. Also notice any statements that you
"hear" only in snatches or very quickly that you didn't realize
were going through your head. A lot of negative, anxiety-arousing
self-talk seems to just "happen," and this kind of self-talk is particularly potent because we aren't *consciously* saying those things
to ourselves.

For instance, you may hear gloomy statements such as, "Things
are never gonna get better" or "I give up," self-critical remarks
such as, "You idiot!" or vague emotional phrases eliciting panic
such as, "Oh no!" If possible, write down the key phrases or sen-
tences you hear in your inner dialogue. You may later be amazed
that you even functioned with all that negativity going on under
the surface.

2. During week two, ask yourself if those mental statements are
reasonable, forgiving, or helpful. If you're not sure, ask yourself
if you would say the same thing to someone you love and want to
succeed. Better yet, ask yourself, "Is this how Jesus would speak
to me?"

Note the phrases that are particularly unkind, destructive, or counterproductive and how they get in the way of problem-solving, parenting, or self-care. Ask yourself where you've heard this kind of talk before and how you may have picked it up from those people in your past. Childhood is an especially critical time, and it's easy to absorb the thinking patterns of parents, teachers, and other influential adults. However, pivotal events in adult life, as well as the attitudes of the people you've spent the most time with, can also influence your thinking patterns without your ever having realized it before going through this process of consciously examining your usual mental "conversations."

If this part is difficult for you—which it will be if you've internalized critical, anxious, or pessimistic voices from others so much that these statements seem permissible to you—ask a friend or therapist what they think of the accuracy, fairness, and helpfulness of those thoughts. There are also some very good books, listed in the reference section of this book, that you can read to get a more objective view of your inner dialogue.

3. During week three, review your list of negative statements and compose—on paper—a counterstatement for each negative statement that you can say as soon as you hear that distressing, discouraging or otherwise unhelpful thought. Begin to talk back to those negative voices that you've internalized somewhere along the way. Be sure that you do so in a way that's believable, however: if it's too bland or Pollyanna-like, you won't sound credible or reasonable, thus your counterthought won't be accepted by your own mind and the negativity will continue.

For instance, if you hear the thought "This situation is intolerable and there's nothing I can do about it," replying "That's not true, everything's fine!" won't work, whereas a rational counterthought such as "Yes, the situation is problematic, but I'm going to find a way to either improve it or better deal with it if that's not possible" will stop the negative talk. Here are two examples of negative thoughts with reasonable positive counterthoughts.

Negative habitual thought: "You've messed up *again*, like you always do." *Counterthought*: "I made a mistake, but I'm going to figure out how and why this happened. And yes, I have 'messed up' in the past, but who hasn't? Also, I reject the judgmental phrase 'like you always do': first, it's not accurate; second, it's not fair or reasonable; and third, I'm changing my negative habits, starting with not listening to that kind of negative self-talk!"

Negative habitual thought: "Oh no, what's going to happen now? I'm so worried; I'm so anxious; this is just awful! I can't deal with this! Oh no . . ." *Counterthought*: "Stop it! Calm down. Take a break if you need it; problems can't be addressed while you're flipping out. I know this situation is worrisome right now, but I insist on stopping this flow of anxiety-producing thoughts. Once I feel calmer, I'll come back to the problem. Don't worry, I'll pray for God's help, and if needed I'll consult with others. For now, I'm going to relax and get my thoughts on a more positive track."

4. During the final week of this thirty-day plan to develop a healthier, happier way of thinking about yourself and responding to the events in your life, *practice*. You've done the background work; now's the time to put it into action, and practice is key. You may want to begin by talking back to yourself in the bathroom mirror. Another strategy for talking back to anxious or critical thoughts is to pretend to be talking on your cell phone when in public. Nobody needs to know that you're talking to yourself.

You may forget now and then, but do try to respond to every negative thought that you hear this week. In a sense, this intense practice is a form of positive "brainwashing," and it's one of the most effective forms of self-care. In fact, habitual negative thoughts can impair even *the capacity* for self-care and self-nurturing, which is what that little girl in you needs and craves.

Keep your lists of negative thoughts and positive counter-thoughts with you at all times, and the instant you hear one of those negative dialogues starting, "talk back" internally (or, if you're alone, out loud if that helps to get the point across). You'll probably have to say your counter-thought many times, and in more than one wording or style, before the automatic negative thoughts stop whirling around in your mind. You may also, depending on the nature of the negative thoughts, have to be very reassuring or very firm, or both. If nothing else works, you may have to initially just say "Stop it!" to yourself when you find yourself becoming self-critical or when you hear doomsday talk beginning in your mind.

At the end of this week, start going through this thirty-day process on an ongoing basis; if you keep at it, you'll become increasingly sensitive to even the quietest, sneakiest little negative thoughts that you may not have noticed when you began listening to yourself. It will then become a positive mental habit in itself: whenever you hear something negative, you'll find yourself mentally composing, or even writing down, a more mature and productive counterthought and zapping that negativity before it brings you down.

As you work your way through these four steps, ask God to guide the way you talk to yourself so that you feel safer, understood, forgiven for past mistakes, and confident that you can make positive changes in your life. If you do this consistently, you'll begin to lighten up on yourself, and you will start to view your situation in a more hopeful light. You'll then more effectively tackle external problems, quiet internal anxieties or self-blaming thoughts, and better enjoy your day. When you slip up—and you will, especially at first—just remind yourself to stop the negative inner chatter and replace it with positive, encouraging self-talk. Everybody wins when you speak to yourself as God would speak to you, his beloved child.

Don't worry about anything; instead, pray about everything.... If you do this, you will experience God's peace, which is far more wonderful than the human mind can understand.

Philippians 4:6–7

So don't get tired of doing what is good. Don't get discouraged and give up, for we will reap a harvest of blessing at the appropriate time.

Galatians 6:9

Give all your worries and cares to God, for he cares about what happens to you.

1 Peter 5:7

Then Jesus said, "Let's get away from the crowds for a while and rest."

Mark 6:31

Dear Lord, please teach me how to take good care of myself. I know that you want the best for me. When I need rest or help or more positive thinking and self-talk, please remind me to stop, reflect, and get back on the right track. Amen.

5

Getting the Support You Need

"How are you doing?"

"Fine, how are you?"

"Fine—have a good one!"

"You too!"

This little exchange, repeated daily in one form or another, reflects the degree to which most of us share our thoughts and feelings as we go through our day at work, on the street, in stores, at the bank, and even at church. It's not that nobody cares, it's a matter of volume: we interact with so many people every day that genuine sharing would be time consuming and "too much" emotionally.

The reason I bring this up isn't to critique our social customs— polite greetings are much better than silence or rudeness—but to highlight the fact that single mothers may have little or no opportunity for meaningful sharing and conversation. We're so focused on meeting the many needs of our children that it's easy to not even notice that we don't have anyone with whom we can regularly exchange ideas and express our emotions.

Lynn is a social worker and single mom who told me with frustration, "In my line of work, you'd think my co-workers would be a great source of support. But they're so busy (or burned out) that they don't want to know what's going on with me or with anyone else in the office. When we're rushing in every morning, we ask routinely, 'How are you?' but if you dare say anything beyond 'Fine,' you get the feeling that you've just stepped on their last nerve. Maybe we give so much all the time that we have nothing left for each other, but the result of this disinterest is that we stay huddled inside closed doors and listen to clients but never to each other.

"By the time I get home, the kids have needs, of course, but all I've done is give without anyone to support me. The children want to tell me about their day, or that they're upset about something, and I try to listen to them while cooking dinner, cleaning up, getting them to do their homework and into bed, you know the drill. On the weekends we have lots of errands and chores to do, and by Sunday night I feel wiped out and dread going to work the next morning to start the whole give-give-give thing again."

Lynn does have a girlfriend she could talk with by phone, but her friend had been depressed lately, so most of the calls involved Lynn listening without sharing yet again. Her family was fairly supportive but lived out of state and didn't get together often. She wondered if she should start telling people at work, "No, I'm *not* 'fine,'" and hope that somebody would care enough to listen. "I'm just so lonely and frustrated with never getting to share anything *real*," she concluded.

After we discussed this lack of support at work, which is something that many single moms face, we decided that Lynn should not even try to get the kind of support she needs from co-workers. Doing so would likely be an exercise in frustration and could even backfire due to unwritten rules such as "Nobody has the emotional 'space' to take on anything above and beyond serving clients' demands." While it's always possible that somebody there feels as she does and that Lynn could develop an after-work relationship that involved more significant sharing, identifying someone and deciding how much to share can be a tricky endeavor. Some workplaces are conducive to leisure time get-togethers, but most are purely work oriented.

This is okay, though, because what single moms like Lynn really need isn't just *any* kind of support but a more freeing and fulfilling support wherein we don't have to carefully censor what we say or how much we disclose about our lives or our children's lives.

As single moms, we do need support outside of work. The question is, how and where can we find that support? We have to take the time to seek people out, join groups we find interesting, or both. We need to make sure that we're available for friendships outside of work, which usually means that we will want to develop our child care network so that we can have "adult time."

Lynn began to realize that she needed time for herself and that a portion of that self-nurturing time could be spent with friends, either individually or in a group—but that this kind of sharing wasn't a realistic option with her co-workers.

Many mothers of younger children enjoy book clubs and similar groups because they can rotate venues, meeting at their own home as well as other members' homes. If your children are older, your options are wider because those who are sufficiently mature and trustworthy can be allowed to stay at home while you meet a friend for lunch, or they can hang out at the mall while you meet with friends in a restaurant on the premises. A good start is to browse online listings for your community or to check the local paper, bookstore schedules, or coffee shop bulletin boards. Some churches have parenting or other special-topic classes or groups, which can be excellent sources of support and potential friendships.

When selecting groups or activities in the interest of meeting people and developing your personal support system, be sure to choose topics that you're genuinely interested in; that way, if you don't happen to meet anyone who interests you, you won't feel that you've wasted your time. If you love painting (or would like to try it), for instance, take a class. If you love to read, join a book club. If you enjoy dancing, take a dance class. Then share a bit of yourself with others, test the waters, and see if anyone with whom you feel some connection reciprocates. Don't be shy—exchange email addresses or phone numbers and set up a time to get together.

Everyone needs friendships and community. If you remain all work and no play, you won't be doing your child or yourself any favors. I know it's hard to schedule extra activities into an already packed schedule, but social support is absolutely essential for your well-being, even if it's just weekly or every other week. When you feel supported, while at work you won't feel deprived, and when you're with your children, you'll have a lot more to give.

Your Self-Care and Support System

Social Support

"No man is an island," the saying goes, but a lot of single mothers feel and act like they are, not because they want to but out of habit or because they feel that depending on others might look like weakness. At school or at work there's little time for more than quick chit-chat or the "How are you?" greeting, and at home there are—well, the kids. Sometimes we do end up sharing things with our children, but this isn't really helpful to us or to them. The single mother–child repartee in the old film *The Goodbye Girl*, for instance, is witty and funny but unrealistic. Our kids aren't prepared to handle adult emotions, and they're biased observers: they love us and want us to be happy, but they're far too young to give us the mature empathy, feedback, or advice we need.

What this means is that unless we make a real effort to schedule in some adult time with friends, relatives, groups, or a counselor, we run the risk of developing practical or psychological problems that we never get a chance to discuss with someone else. This lack of an outlet for sharing perspectives and feelings can result in our missing problems that need our attention. We may have a vague sense that difficulties in areas such as finances or child care are escalating, but when we're too self-contained we may fail to notice how unsatisfactory those situations are becoming.

The psychological problems that go unrecognized and un-talked through are equally if not more important. Without an outside perspective, it's tempting to rely only on our own impulses or opinions and thus make whichever decision first occurs to us without really analyzing the situation and considering our options. Because it's so challenging for single moms to find the time or freedom for leisurely, intimate conversations with friends or advisors, we're more likely to make snap decisions or to spiral further into a negative mood.

Examples of psychological problems that can worsen in this way are frequent bouts of anxiety, depression, anger, fatigue, or stress. But these are only a sampling of the areas in which we can run amuck when we tough it out alone for too long, particularly if the seeds of future vulnerabilities or distorted thinking were sown during childhood and have never been addressed. For instance, if your father was domineering or abusive, you may be more prone to depression and anxiety after months of dealing with a supervisor who's critical or has a hot temper.

This is especially likely for those mothers who had children when they were young and never had the time or opportunity to get the help they needed to heal from painful childhood experiences. If we don't invest the time and resources necessary to grow and mature, we can fall into a reactive stance. This habitual tendency reflects a lack of self-understanding and self-care, which in turn makes it difficult to pause and take stock of a situation, perceive our true feelings about it, and respond constructively rather than in a reactive, knee-jerk manner.

Getting social support—from friends, relatives, co-workers, church members, or neighbors—is essential for a balanced state

> **The Bright Side of Single Mothering**
>
> If tension existed between your child's father and your own extended family, you can often reverse this. His absence at gatherings will reduce conflict so that those important relationships can be easier or renewed. (Holidays can be a lot nicer too.)

of mind and a healthy sense of connectedness with others. Some of us need a lot, some of us need relatively little, but we all need at least some regular human contact that's supportive in nature.

When we're in charge of our families, we must take care of our children and manage our households, in addition to working at jobs we may or may not like. This requires a great deal of focus and energy and can be stressful and isolating at times. Because you may have to keep your nose to the grindstone much of the time, having friends, relatives, ministers, or others with whom you can talk honestly about what's going on and how you're feeling is vitally important. As a single mother, you can spend so much time giving to others and doing what needs to be done that you can easily feel depleted or get stuck in one perspective. Though it can be challenging to make the time for it, you do need to nurture and maintain supportive relationships in order to replenish your energy and spirit. We all need a supportive network of people with whom we can exchange caring attention and concern about the little details as well as the important issues in our lives.

Aim for Balance between Time with Friends and Time Alone

It's easy to determine when you're getting too much or too little social support. When there's too much, you feel connected but are socializing so much that you have no time to spend alone in quiet reading, reflection, or just sitting outside. When there's too little, you will begin to feel isolated, lonely, and "bottled up" emotionally. If thoughts and feelings have accumulated inside and you have nobody to share them with so you can hear a fresh perspective, you'll begin to feel burdened or "stuck." Talking with trusted friends can help you to relax and feel the relief of shifting your attention for a while to what's going on in *their* lives; in so doing, you will also be helping and supporting your friend.

What's healthy and refreshing is a balance of time alone and time with others. Sometimes just being around people can help, but you'll probably find that you need some real sharing time as well—time together with people who are interested in some of the same things you're interested in and who enjoy giving and receiving support. If this is new for you, start taking baby steps toward supportive connection by inviting someone for coffee or lunch on a regular basis. It's easy to fall into the grind of working at your job and trying to be a supermom at home, but if this continues too long, supermom will soon feel more like super-burned-out mom.

Aim for a balanced social life, even if all you do is attend a monthly book club or have bagels and coffee with a friend every other week. Even if your time feels too limited for such outings, keep in mind that you'll feel more healthy and balanced when you have the right amount of social connection.

Professional Support

In some cases, ongoing feelings of being overwhelmed or chronically tired can mask underlying depression or anxiety. At such times it is essential to seek professional help. If you've been feeling distressed for a long time (for example, mildly depressed, irritable, nervous, distractible, exhausted, or unable to concentrate), you may not see those feelings as a problem requiring extra help: you're so used to feeling that way that it no longer alarms you, and you can't remember feeling any other way.

On the other hand, you may accurately notice a big change in yourself that raises red flags for you. You may have tried to "get over it" or "snap out of it" but haven't been able to do so. This can be perplexing, because often there is no one event to which you can point and say, "Ah, yes, that was what caused me to get depressed." More often a low-level anxious, depressed, or pessimistic mood will creep up on you, then settle down and make itself at home. Trying with all your might to evict this unwanted guest, you may have read self-help books, tried not to think about how you feel, or distracted yourself with workaholism or busyness. You might have even used alcohol or other drugs to self-medicate the feelings away.

None of these, however, will be effective. If you've tried but failed to get yourself out of an enduring mood that is threatening your productivity and interfering with your ability to feel happy and hopeful and you still feel "stuck" in this way, ask your doctor for help and for referrals, seek help at a counseling center, or call a mental health hotline to get started. But do get the professional care you need right away. Once you feel better you'll be glad you advocated for your own well-being, and your children will benefit from a happier, calmer mom.

Child Care Support

One of the most essential needs for successful single motherhood is a reliable support network. Notice that I said "support network," not simply "support system," which you may think of as emotionally supportive friends. They're important too, but they may not be willing or able to watch your child when you have an emergency or need a night free to study, catch up with repairs or bill paying, or just relax.

Others think of a support system as just one person, usually a grandmother who's willing to help out with child care. Even for married couples this isn't enough. For single parents, it's woefully inadequate. Don't let shyness or financial limitations prevent you from developing this essential network. You need a reliable network in order to cover all the bases, be prepared, and feel secure. Your children need it too.

Kelly, an ambitious twenty-eight-year-old human resources specialist, had been working full time while taking an online class to further her career. Most of the time she felt capable of juggling these responsibilities as a single mother of Ethan, her six-year-old. With homework on top of her day job, however, her child care needs had increased. "Ethan's an easygoing boy and just loves being with my sister Renee, who's single and free in the evenings. She watches him whenever I have a work deadline or need a big chunk of study time. But here's the problem—she's moving across the country to take a new job in a couple of months, I have no other family around, and I can't afford a babysitter every time I need to cram for an exam. What will I do when Renee's gone?"

Kelly had been very lucky thus far, because in a sense she'd been operating without a safety net. Notwithstanding her sister's upcoming move, Kelly's child care arrangements hadn't been adequate for a number of reasons:

1. Even with her sister willing and able to help, what happens when Kelly's sole child care supporter gets sick or has a prior commitment? This is a common single-parent situation: putting all one's eggs in one basket, only to find there's a hole in it! Having real deadlines and other work to do but no child care is a common source of stress, and it can be avoided by making sure you have a number of sources to call upon, whether paid for or bartered with exchanged child care.
2. Kelly probably tried not to ask for help as often as needed because she didn't want to impose unduly on her sister— hence she wasn't really getting enough studying time. Her social life and energy level were likely suffering too.
3. She had no "net" for those times when a genuine emergency may have developed and she wasn't able to reach her sister.
4. While her son enjoyed spending time with Kelly's sister, no other children were present, thus Ethan had no opportunity

for the occasional child care swap in which built-in play was a bonus. This social aspect of child care isn't necessary all the time (the undivided attention of a caring adult such as Kelly's sister is wonderful for a younger child), but the occasional playdate or sleepover is both fun and enriching for your child.

5. Most telling regarding her urgent need for a new and larger child care network, Kelly had asked, "What will I do when Renee's gone?" but the wiser question would be, "What can I do *before* Renee's gone?"

As a single mother, you need a reliable child care network. This isn't an option—it's essential. As you're developing your own child care network, think of an actual net, like the ones that trapeze artists use in case they fall. The net is strong and reliable because it's formed from all the knots connecting the rope in regular intervals. In like manner, your support network should include a number of people with whom you can exchange child care, sleepovers, and the like. It should include people you can call, in urgent situations, even at the last minute. Ideally these individuals will come from diverse areas of your life: friends; neighbors; parents of your child's classmates; people from your church, school, or job; and so on. As investment counselors will tell you, you should "diversify your portfolio."

What criteria should you look for when cultivating your child care support network? The first and most important, of course, is safety and dependability. Even if someone is loads of fun and great with kids, if your instinct tells you that he or she is a bit too "flaky" to keep a steady eye on your child, has a tendency to leave hazardous objects around the house, or tends to get carried away at the computer or on the phone, count that person out. This isn't to say that everyone in your network must childproof their entire home and literally watch your child at every moment, but you do need to gauge their level of alertness and common sense with respect to the age and needs of your child.

Of course it should go without saying that any evidence or strong intuitive sense you get about someone regarding drinking, drug use, sexual inappropriateness, and other serious problems rules him or her out as part of your support network.

Developing your child care support network will require a time investment up front but will be well worth it over the long haul. Be sure to offer child care to other moms, married or single, who could use some child-free time as well. Friendships often deepen when we exchange child care because we are demonstrating we trust the other person with our precious children. If you take good care of yourself, reaching out to make friends even if you're on the shy side, you'll also feel healthier and more balanced. In so doing, you can offer your own kindness and support to other parents. Remember, the team approach helps everybody involved, as long as you use discernment and reciprocity. For single moms especially, a strong child care network is a win-win situation.

Don't forget to show hospitality to strangers, for some who have done this have entertained angels without realizing it!

Hebrews 13:2

A friend is always loyal, and a brother is born to help in time of need.

Proverbs 17:17

Help her in every way you can, for she has helped many in their needs, including me.

Romans 16:2

Don't think only about your own affairs, but be interested in others, too, and what they are doing.

Philippians 2:4

God, I know that I cannot do everything for myself and my children on my own strength. Please fortify me in body and spirit, and help me to reach out to you and to other people, both to help them and to be helped by them, so that we will all feel safe and supported. Amen.

6

Getting Organized

A single mother's need to be organized boils down to simple math: what two married parents do, one single parent must do. This goes for household, paperwork, and scheduling organization—the Big Three that either help us in our busy lives because they're orderly and systematized or act as annoyances that trip us up again and again. Few people are naturally organized in all three areas. Some people were raised in chaotic or messy homes and never learned the basic skills of organizing and setting up effective systems in the first place.

What this means is that to improve our sense of calm and of being in control, we may first have to learn the "how" of organizing our households, our paperwork, and our time.

Sarah is a teacher and single mom who loves planning weekend outings and activities with her son and daughter, ages six and eight. During relaxed times they all enjoyed each other's company. The same couldn't be said, however, during workdays when efficient organization and timeliness were needed. Sarah was tired of all the rushing around every morning as she tried to get the children and herself out of the house in time for school and work. She confided that on school mornings, and often during the evening dinner-homework-bathtime rush, she's "a different person," watching the clock and barking out commands or yelling in frustration.

"I've tried setting my alarm earlier and earlier in the mornings to help us get a head start and avoid being late, but then I'm more tired and the kids don't want to get out of bed. And of course things are never where they're supposed to be, which adds to my stress level. I can't afford a housekeeper, and my kids are pretty young—any ideas? I hate it when our days start (and sometimes end) with me nagging, running around, pushing them to hurry. They end up feeling stressed too. When I get home and check the mail, I get 'past due' notices because I couldn't find the cable bill, and then there are late fees—it never ends!"

What Sarah described is typical for working parents with children, whether married or not. The difference for single moms, though, is that we have to corral the kids, accomplish the tasks, find the materials, and stick to the schedules all by ourselves. We all have those times when nothing works smoothly and chaos ensues. Sarah was concerned about the quality of her time with the kids on work/school days; she didn't want stress to take over their relationships or to spoil the day for any of them. Nobody wants to start a day at school or at work feeling rattled and overwhelmed.

Sarah had already begun trying new techniques (getting up earlier) to prevent these problems from happening in the first place. That's a good start, but as CEO of her family, she needed to step back and evaluate precisely where the glitches were occurring, which factors were leading to all the last-minute rushing around, how disorganization was contributing to the problem, and so on. Then and only then could she plan a "turnaround" for her family so that even on busy days she could feel calm and in control, enjoy her children, and have the confidence that they—and mom—were beginning and ending each day in a positive way.

More Organized, Less Stressed

Most of us have weaknesses in some area of our lives; usually one seems almost continual and is distressing. What are your weak areas in terms of organization and time management? When I ask this question, most people can answer without hesitation and often with a great deal of frustration because they've tried many times to improve. You know what that's like—you make a solemn oath to yourself to never, ever lose your car keys again, yet on a morning when you're rushing around to get to work, take your child to school or to an appointment, or both, the game begins: looking here, looking there, watching the time slip away, and wanting to scream because the keys are nowhere in sight.

Often we do improve for a while after watching a how-to show or reading an article on getting organized. This makes it all the more maddening when we find ourselves slipping back into old patterns again. We lose the keys *again*, we don't get our child ready in time to make the bus *again*, or we forget to pay that bill and get hit with late fees *again*.

Let's face it, sometimes it's all just too much for any one person to do!

A Strategy for Getting Organized That Works

I've described the basic steps toward achieving reliable organization of your home and your paperwork below. Before you begin getting your world into good order, keep in mind that (1) you'll probably need to set aside several (or many) blocks of time over a few days or weeks, and (2) nobody else can organize your life for you. Even if you're lucky enough to get help with this task from a friend or a professional organizer, getting totally organized will require your decisions about what to keep, throw away, or give away and your realistic appraisal of storage and systems that will and won't work for you.

I've seen professional organizers (available for hire in many cities) help people organize their papers and complex projects—only to have it all fall apart shortly after the organizer finishes the job. This is what happens when you don't first analyze your habits and inclinations, your likes and dislikes (more on this below), but try to copy the techniques and supplies that someone else finds useful or that you've seen in a magazine or book but that aren't really pleasing to you or don't fit with your personality and lifestyle.

Developing workable systems and better organization is more fun when you're open-minded and creative; in fact, creativity is what can make this otherwise dreary, time-consuming task more pleasant, even *fun*. So think "outside the box" when you're ready to get more organized. It's far better to devise an unusual system that you and/or your child can maintain—and even enjoy maintaining—than to set up one that looks conventional but simply won't work long-term.

Here's an example. Closets are traditionally where people place their shoes, and many shoe storage gadgets are manufactured for this purpose. Trouble is, for many active families, this system doesn't actually work day to day: shoes end up kicked off at the front door, scattered around the family room, or pushed under the bed where they may never be seen again. My older daughter got me started on a great shoe storage technique that works for me (and believe me, I've bought all sorts of shoe organizers and have lectured myself, all to no avail). She realistically appraised the situation, then set up a wooden rack for large shoes and a basket for her children's shoes *right by the front door.*

How much smarter this is than working against human nature by insisting that shoes be immediately carried back to all those bedroom closets, day after day! An added benefit is that because the storage items are so conveniently placed and easy to use, the children as well as the adults have no problem putting away their

---

The Ostrich Syndrome

Causes: easily pressed panic button; disorganization; helplessness/giving up; depression; abject fear; wishful thinking/overly optimistic mind-set; procrastination; growing up in a financially fearful home (lack or constant fear of lack/doom).

Consequences: continuing/escalating procrastination and disorganization; chronic worry; unable to open bills; late fees, collection notices, litigation threats; lowered sense of effectiveness/confidence; damaged self-image/self-esteem.

---

shoes. Even better, they never end up with a missing shoe on busy mornings or have to grope around under beds looking for it.

This example illustrates one of the organization types described below, of which I was long a member: Partially Organized. When my children were young we lived in Boston where mittens, gloves, hats, and scarves were essential many months of the year. The number of items per person was impressive, as we'd come home wet from melting snow or rain, and thus needed multiple sets. With several family members, the quantity of cold-weather gear was truly astounding. Thus, I came up with the idea of baskets and drying racks at the front door, which solved last-minute problems we had on school mornings when, for instance, only one glove could be found.

I mention this to emphasize that we can be very good at keeping one area of our lives organized and stress-free (in my case, winter item storage), yet have ongoing frustration and messiness in another area because we've never figured out or accepted our real-life habits and thus haven't set up systems that we'll all *use* (for me, shoe racks/ baskets). You may be able to think of areas in your life—whether it's paperwork, finances, kitchenware, clothing, toys, etc.—that are trouble free and of others that are in constant disarray.

The key is to let go of the "shoulds" (particularly when it comes to the way we "should" clean or organize), and start thinking like a "human factors psychologist." Human factors psychologists know that fighting engrained habits or human nature is a losing cause, so they create systems that people can and will utilize, regardless of their current energy level or mood.

Such psychologists have consulted, for example, for fast-food restaurant owners who need customers to pick up after themselves. The psychologist first watches what people actually do with their trash and trays, then designs spaces that are easy to keep clean. With this knowledge, they design spacious trash containers and convenient places to stack trays, locating them in places that make it easier for customers—even those who are lazy or in a hurry—to dump their trash and stack their trays than to put them on counters or leave them on tables. Once you adopt this nonjudgmental "human factors" approach, you'll be able to redesign your paperwork systems and your home in ways that help you and your child keep things tidy without constant arguing or reminding and without ongoing messiness and frustration.

Amy's Story: Victory over the "Clothes Chair"

Amy, a CPA and single mother with whom I worked in counseling, said that her work was hard enough, but adding her after-work parenting responsibilities left her feeling frazzled and forgetful much of the time. As we analyzed the situation further, she realized that one of her biggest stressors was living in a messy home—and the biggest offender, as it turns out, wasn't her child but Amy herself!

As a CPA, Amy was good at home finances and paperwork. She and her daughter had worked out a good system for keeping the kitchen clean, and the bathroom was seldom a problem. After going through the Single Mother's Inventory (see chapter 2) and examining her life, she noticed an area that was a chronic source of frustration to her: for whatever reason, she simply could not get herself to hang up her clothes after a demanding day at work and a tiring commute. Day after day, week after week, month after month, Amy mentally lectured and chastised herself for throwing her suits, blouses, and slacks on various chairs, where wrinkly piles seemed to work as magnets for the next evening's clothing.

Finally Amy stepped back from the situation, observed her habits for a few days, then asked herself, "Okay, Amy, if you won't hang your clothes up in the closet where they belong every night, what *would* you be willing to do that would keep the room neater and prevent wrinkles or extra dry cleaning?" Almost immediately, she heard a tired little voice answer in her mind, "Well, I'd be willing to hang them on a hook, a nail, *anything* other than trudging up to that closet, opening the door, checking them to see if they need washing, then hanging them up."

Amy considered this option briefly, but she knew it wasn't realistic since nails or hooks could damage her clothes. Still, surely *something* could be worked out between Amy and her weary inner child. Out of ideas, one Saturday Amy browsed in a home supply store, wondering which storage items might work. She'd ask herself, "Would you be willing to use this?" This felt a little silly, and she finally settled on two over-the-door racks that wouldn't damage her work clothes, but would keep them off chairs and prevent wrinkles.

Once at home, she placed the racks on two doors on the first floor, and—lo and behold—her clothes were never piled up again, looking messy and getting so wrinkled that they required extra cleanings. Each weekend she simply transferred the clothes to the closet, the clothes hamper, or the dry cleaner. By each Monday morning, her clothes were in great shape, neatly hung or folded and a lot more pleasant to select and coordinate. This system worked because it was designed to accommodate *her*, rather than vice versa.

You can use this approach to get control of clutter both for you and for your child. Like a human factors psychologist, analyze your storage and cleaning systems, be creative, and design systems for cleaning, organizing, and upkeep that don't fight human nature but instead *make it easier and quicker to be tidy and orderly than not.*

Financial Organization

Make sure you review each of your financial goals, payments due, and the like and write down one next action that will get you going. You'd be amazed how this simple shift can change your life and get even the most stubborn financial boulders moving again. On monthly bills such as your credit card, cable or internet, rent or mortgage, cell phone, student loans, and so on, it can be a big relief to have them taken out of your checking account automatically if you have a sufficient financial cushion (at least one month's worth of total bills).

If you don't have enough financial cushion in your account to be sure there will be enough money to cover automatic bill-pay debits, there's an equally reliable technique to relieve your brain of constantly trying to remember due dates and to make sure you never get those awful late fees: list the due dates of every single bill in the back of your appointment book, then go through every month ahead, placing a reminder to pay each bill at least five to seven days before the actual due date. If your income fluctuates significantly, such that some months you have more money than others, or if your paychecks or support payments arrive irregularly, you may want to place the reminders even further in advance, say ten to fifteen days; that way you can still take your mind off the issue for at least a couple of weeks each month, confident that you'll have a good two weeks to arrange the money you'll need to pay the bills.

Remember, even if you have money concerns, and most of us do, you shouldn't have to worry about them 24–7. If you make a habit of advance planning, you can give the financial part of your brain a rest, *and* you'll have fair warning when money is running low.

> **The Bright Side of Single Mothering**
>
> Your home can be more orderly because you're not waiting for your spouse to do his share and/or vice versa; you have more clarity regarding who's doing what, and often it's simply easier to know that you'll take care of tasks yourself without arguing or begging a spouse to help.

In addition to magazine articles and books on the subject, there are many excellent audio books on organizing your life, which you can listen to while commuting or cleaning house. A number are listed in the Recommended Reading section at the end of this book. I hope you'll take advantage of these resources, because once you feel that you're fully in control of the aggravating details in your life, including household chores and financial paperwork, you'll free up a lot of energy and will feel much more in control of your life.

Home Organization

For most people, finances and paperwork are the most pressing areas to get organized because lapses in attention to bills and deadlines can result in negative consequences such as late fees, overdraft charges, harassing letters, or calls from creditors. When it comes to home organization, the negative consequences of chronic disorder come not from the outside world but from within your mind—stress, frustration, and that "Oh, not again!" feeling. Too much clutter can also affect your child, who may appear indifferent or lazy when in reality he or she lacks the skills or equipment needed to study in a space conducive to good concentration (or to "clean your room right now!"). Disorganization can likewise affect your family life, creating stress when it causes you or the children to run late for school or work because shoes, homework, or car keys can't be found or when you end up burning dinner because you can't find the oven mitt or spatula. Humble though

> Give a child a specific quota: "Please pick up five things." This is easier to manage than being told to clean up an entire room, and kids enjoy counting the items that they put away.
>
> Gail Reichlin and Caroline Winkler, *The Pocket Parent*[1]

it may sound when compared to working or financial matters, home organization is important for your mental health and your enjoyment of time spent at home. It can also improve your child's life by making it easier to study or do homework, get chores done, and avoid those rushed mornings that result in a stressful start to the school day.

The point of increasing your home organization is not to impress the neighbors or live up to glossy magazine images of homes where nobody (certainly not children or teenagers!) actually *lives*. The point of having greater order and better systems in your household is not to slave away in pursuit of perfection or to make your child dread the phrase "clean your room." The point is to free up your mind and your time, making it easier and more convenient to keep your home and lives orderly than to let things go and live with clutter or disorganization.

Which Organization/Cleaning Type Are You?

When evaluating your current home-care satisfactions and frustrations, ask yourself how you currently approach cleaning and organizing. Determine where you currently fit in the following categories. Remember, there's no need for any self-recrimination or guilt because any weak areas are probably due to habits you learned from others long ago or are the result of inadequate supplies and systems. Here are the categories:

1. **Generally Organized**: Your home is rarely messy because you grew up with good organizational techniques that you

learned from your parents. You don't have to think much about this part of your life, and your living space stays adequately neat and organized. You love a streamlined home and clean or reorganize on a regular basis. You don't let things get too messy or cluttered, but neither do you try to tackle too much at a time.

Result: Because you have a good system in place and do little maintenance actions in an ongoing way, your home may not be perfect, but it's rarely a disaster zone. You've probably taught your child how to do his or her share without expecting too much and by making it easy to keep things reasonably tidy.

2. **Generally Disorganized**: Your home is pretty cluttered but you're used to it. It doesn't bother you (consciously, anyway) because you don't "see" it anymore, except for those times when you can't find the bowl you need, lose your keys, or trip over toys and shoes, all of which happen frequently. Since nothing you've tried thus far has helped long term, you try to just work around the messes until that magical "someday" when you're going to figure out how to get it all cleaned up.

Result: Your living spaces are never pleasing to look at and are demoralizing if you allow yourself to notice or think about all the "stuff" that seems to gather out of nowhere. If you do engage in a massive clean sweep, it's an exhausting experience that rarely feels finished even after tons of time and energy spent; this is why you try to "not notice" the messes. Getting your child to do chores around the house may feel like a losing cause and ends up in yelling, threats of consequences, or pleading. You probably haven't noticed until now that your child doesn't have the needed skills or equipment to keep things clean and organized—and that you don't either.

3. **Partially Organized**: If this is you, certain rooms in your home are well maintained—say, the bathroom—while others are often a mess (kitchens, bedrooms, and family rooms are big offenders). You'd love to keep every room tidy, but this seems an impossible dream no matter what you do. You're irritated by clutter and disorganization, and every now and then you go on a massive cleaning streak, after which you're physically spent; when things pile up again you understandably dread the next huge cleaning spree.

Result: Your living space stays neat in some areas but regularly becomes an intolerable mess in others. Your child may be good at picking up after him or herself in some areas but may not know how to clean other parts of the house and may lack the proper supplies to do so. You may never have really thought through what's needed to make your problem areas easier to organize and maintain.

General Guidelines for Getting and Keeping Your Home Organized

First, acknowledge which of the three home-maintenance categories above reflects your habitual approach. If you're generally organized, you're probably interested only in little tips to enhance your current systems. If you're generally disorganized or partly/sometimes organized, you're probably eager to learn how to get your life and household running more smoothly—if so, read on.

Next, when you have some free time, go through your home with a pad and pen, jotting down every single area that's a cleaning or organizing challenge. Take a leisurely, nonjudgmental approach and list every problem you see, major or minor, as a human factors psychologist would.

Be as specific as you can. For example, write "kitchen: dirty dishes piled on the counter," "hall closet: total wreck, all sorts of things in there, can barely shut the door," or "bedroom: clothes piled on chair, huge stack of unopened mail on the dresser." Be sure to relax as you do this, because you don't need to *do* anything about the problems right now. Merely record the "hot spots" that attract clutter or are stubbornly messy.

When you feel ready, go through the same areas with pen and paper in hand once again, brainstorming ideas for storage supplies or systems to tackle the items that have migrated into the wrong places. Banish any "shoulds" (for example, "I should stop leaving my clothes on the chair after work," or "My son should hang up his towels after his bath," or "We should stop leaving our shoes wherever we happen to sit down first"). "Shoulds" may sound noble, but they rarely lead to change because they lead to more pressure on yourself or your child; resistance and guilt won't improve the situation, but creative thinking and smarter strategizing will.

Instead of declaring what you or your child *should* do, say to yourself, "Okay, this is a problem that's bothered me for a while, and nothing I've tried has changed the situation. I'm now going to look at the problem from a different angle: what *would* make it easier to avoid this problem?" Then ask yourself creative questions that will help you to consider every possible idea, whether standard or silly, that might work. Here are some examples to get you started:

- "When I get home, tired after a day at work, what would help me to put my clothes somewhere other than the chair?"
- "Can my son easily reach the towel rod, or is it a bit too high for him, making it tempting for him to leave wet towels on the floor?"
- "Do I have too much stuff to keep track of, things that I could donate or throw away if I dedicated a day or two to each category such as clothes, books, magazines, and toys?"

87

- "Do we have an easy dish-washing system, or are dishes constantly piling up because we have inconvenient supplies or setups, making this more of a hassle than it needs to be?"
- "Are the kitchen cabinets organized so that the children can help with putting things away and so that we can find what we need without a lot of rummaging around, bending over, or climbing on chairs?"

Feast or Famine Organization, Cleaning, and Maintenance

To keep your home organized and reasonably pleasant to the eyes, avoid what I call the "feast or famine" approach, which many of us have grown up with and may be stuck in now, not realizing that there's a better way. As single mothers, we have enough to do without adding to our stress levels with this tiring and unsatisfying approach consisting of (1) letting things go until we can't stand it any more, (2) going on cleaning and organizing "benders," taking our kids along on these ambitious campaigns to get the whole house clean in one Saturday, or every weekend, then (3) letting things go until the next time we get overwhelmed by the mess. The feast or famine approach provides us with episodes of orderliness for a day or two or even longer, followed by stretches of time in which we try to tolerate increasing clutter, piled up clothes, dishes, unopened mail, and general yuckiness.

A better approach to household maintenance:

1. *Make it easy to be orderly*: Focus on fixing systems and supplies, not people.
2. *Do a little at a time, on a regular basis*: Focus on reorganizing your home so that it's usually pleasant and convenient with minimal but frequent pick-ups, put-aways, and wipe-ups.

3. *Stagger deep cleaning tasks*: To preserve energy and motivation for you and your child, schedule sections of your home to tidy up or clean each week, month, or longer (thorough floor cleaning, window washing, reorganizing closets, etc.).

If you're generally organized, you're in great shape and may not need any improvement in this area. If you're generally or partially disorganized, you may or may not realize what a hassle it is to live in a chaotic environment; it's likely that you grew up in a home that was cluttered or difficult to keep clean.

If you're not naturally an organized person, or if as a child you lived in a rather disorganized home, you may need to say many, many prayers as you go through this transformative process. God will help you to focus on what needs to be done next, come up with creative solutions, and find just the book, friend, software, or other resource to help you reconfigure your home and financial systems for minimum stress and maximum calm.

Commit your work to the LORD, and then your plans will succeed.

Proverbs 16:3

Then the LORD said to Moses, "Why are you crying out to me? Tell the people to get moving!"

Exodus 14:15

Well done, my good and faithful servant. You have been faithful in handling this small amount, so now I will give you many more responsibilities.

Matthew 25:21

Be strong and courageous, and do the work. Don't be afraid or discouraged by the size of the task, for the LORD God, my God, is with you. He will not fail you or forsake you. He will see to it that all the work . . . is finished correctly.

1 Chronicles 28:20

Lord, I want to become more organized and orderly in all aspects of my life, and I ask for your encouragement every step of the way. Please guide me to helpful people, books, and ideas to assist and inspire me whenever I feel stuck. Help me to think in innovative ways to fulfill our daily responsibilities with greater reliability and ease. Amen.

7

Your Money, Your Job, and Your Dreams

We all need money to survive, to grow, and to pursue our goals. Our children need financial security, which, of course, depends on our own. When you're a single mother, the need for an adequate income and savings cushion for unexpected expenses is acute. While I've met a single mom or two with trust funds and generous inheritances, most of us must work for a living. On the plus side, working hard keeps us active and sharp. As a group, we tend to be hardworking, self-sufficient, and dedicated to providing for our children, no matter what it requires of us.

The challenge is knowing that "the buck stops here," figuratively and literally, especially if we're not making as much money as we'd like or if the work we do is unsatisfying. The goal of this chapter is to help you step back, get some perspective, and evaluate your financial situation, how well your income meets your family's needs, and how closely your work reflects your talents and aspirations.

When we become single mothers, many if not most of us experience "sticker shock" because suddenly, even if we receive child support, the family income decreases such that it's equal to or lower than our expenses. As you probably know all too well, studies have repeatedly found that after divorce, the man's income tends to rise while the woman's tends to fall. This has a lot to do with what the mother was doing prior to the divorce. While many were working full time, some were working part time or were stay-at-home moms. This increased financial stress is also associated with what the mother is doing to earn a living after the divorce: she may not have the experience and skills for high-income jobs, and the costs of raising children single-handedly, particularly if paid child care is necessary, can sap previously adequate salaries.

Thus, most single mothers have money on their minds and are focused on finding ways to provide for their children's wants and needs while maintaining adequate savings. Single moms realize that they must be vigilant about money because other people depend on them. Whether or not a single mom is prepared for the task of providing for her family or even wants to become an ambitious go-getter in the workforce, she's got to somehow bring in sufficient income for her family. But this necessity doesn't mean she must give up on her dreams—what's required is getting clear about her current situation, getting smart about viable career options, and getting strategic about planning for her family's needs in the future.

Jennifer, an office supervisor who was widowed five years ago, sighed, "I'm absolutely miserable in my job but have no idea how I'll ever get out of it. I'm a single mother so I can't take chances on this job market, but every day is so stressful that I'm pretty useless for the kids at least an hour or two after I get home. I feel so bad about this because they deserve better, but sometimes I just come in the door, throw my keys on the table, and tell them I need to lie down for a while. I have to give them credit because nowadays they *do* leave me alone. I can't blame them—who'd *want* to talk to me in my after-work state?

"My income is okay, but this isn't the kind of work I'd hoped to do; it's just the best I could come up with when we really needed the money. Now I'm stuck in a job I hate, I'm no good as a mother by five o'clock, and every day I feel too wiped out to look for another job. I don't know what to do, but this can't go on forever—I hope."

Jennifer was in a stuck phase, but that didn't mean she was permanently stuck. A stuck phase is one in which you know that your job isn't good for you or doesn't bring in enough money, but you can't afford to take time off or quit in order to look for a better position, take classes, or otherwise improve your career. If you're in a similar situation, you'll feel much better if you remind yourself that stuck phases have a beginning, a middle, and an end—that is, if you're determined to improve your life. True, your options may be limited for immediate change, but the future—quite possibly much sooner than you think—holds promise for a means of providing for yourself and your family that is healthier, more rewarding, and more authentically suited to who you are.

Fortunately, Jennifer was able to reconsider her words, "I don't know what to do, but this can't go on forever—I hope." Though it sounds despairing, the seeds of positive change were right there in her own words: she *knew* she didn't want to stay in that job, she wanted something better, and she hoped that the situation would improve—she just didn't know how to go about it. As a single mother, she was wisely avoiding impulsive changes that could jeopardize her children's security, but she recognized that it would be easier to be the kind of mom she wanted to be once she was on a healthier path, which could start with finding a job more in keeping with her interests and talents.

Your Money

Single mothers need several levels of income and available cash for daily use, for making sure their bills can be paid on time, and for accumulating an adequate savings cushion for emergencies and unforeseen expenses (ever noticed that the car *only* needs repair when you're short on cash?). Here are the basics, which you're probably already familiar with but you may find helpful to reevaluate regarding your current financial situation.

1. Your financial cushion: As a single mom, you need a "cushion" that will absorb most financial shocks—unexpected car repairs, tax bills, school fees, plumbing disasters, dental costs, and all those other money drains that occur when you can least afford them—without causing you to have a panic attack or to do without the basics. If you don't currently make much money or if you've never been good at budgeting, this can seem daunting at first. One of the best ways to obtain a cushion to help you feel more secure is to have your bank automatically withdraw a small amount of money into a savings account each month—an amount that you won't notice or miss.

Another trick that's surprisingly effective is to open another account at a different bank with free checking that isn't convenient for you to make withdrawals or debit purchases, then have an automatic "bill pay" set up that will deposit money from your main account into that one each month. I've used both of these systems; they're great because when you don't notice the money withdrawn, or when it's just too much trouble to make a trek down to the "inconvenient" bank (many smaller banks offer free checking) to make a withdrawal, the money stays put.

Once you get these started, it's time for some "selective amnesia": condition yourself to "forget" where your little stockpile is building. If all you're doing is putting money in, you don't need to check the balances. Tell yourself that all you have is your main banking account. Trust me, you'll remember whenever you really need the cash.

If money is *really* tight for you right now, here's yet another tactic for building up your cushion: anytime you get change, especially silver (nickels, dimes, and quarters), empty it from your purse into a child's piggy bank that has no pre-cut opening at the bottom; many of the cheaper plastic piggy banks are constructed without any way to empty them without cutting them open. This is another smart use of the "too much trouble" factor to save money. My father did this with a large, ugly, pink piggy bank I gave him as a joke when my oldest daughter was a baby. I had no idea he routinely put all his spare quarters in there, but the amount of money when it was full was astonishing—hundreds of dollars!

2. Short-term goals: Once your cushion is in place, you're going to feel a lot more secure. Now it's time to set some short-term goals. Susan Reynolds and Lauren Bakken write in *One-Income Household: How to Do a Lot with a Little*, "Short-term goals are manageable goals you can achieve in a relatively short amount of time. Paying down all your credit card debt, paying off a furniture or car loan, and establishing a savings account to cover your emergency fund or to pay for a new refrigerator are all short-term goals. As long as you create them and set a viable deadline for achieving them, you're on the right track."[1] They note, "Short-term goals should be:

- Specific: Be clear and straightforward when setting short-term goals and break them down into their smallest denominator to increase the likelihood of meeting them.
- Measurable: Make sure they provide quantifiable, visible results within a self-determined, relatively short time frame.
- Attainable: You want to reach a little, but not so far that you can't meet them relatively quickly.

- Valuable: If your goals are in alignment with your values, you'll feel good about working toward them.
- Progressive: They should advance your long-term goals or build upon each other to advance your cause.
- Primary: Start with those that will guarantee success and motivate you to solidify a practice of setting and achieving short-term goals."[2]

3. Long-term goals: Long-term goals are focused on enhancing your future security or happiness. It's important to realize that goals that are short-term for some people may be longer-term for others due to their circumstances. If you've got a lot of debt or if your income is far too low right now to even think about replacing your car or even your refrigerator, or if you'd love to start your own business one day but you probably won't have the funds for several years, put these wish lists in your long-term financial goals list.

We all have different resources, but what we have in common is the need for financial security and the need to have and pursue our dream, both for ourselves and for our children. These two needs are the drivers for our long-term financial goals. Reynolds and Bakken explain that "Everyone needs a dream. Your one-income household must have both a game plan for immediate needs and a vision for long-term needs, wants, or desires. Long-term goals can be the compass that keeps you on course."[3]

Whether you have a lot of money, too little, or just barely enough, you need an emergency cushion that's not easy to dip into when you or the kids have a whim for some indulgence (and we *all* have such whims). You also need short-term goals that are doable in the coming months or year and provide satisfaction and increase your motivation when they are fulfilled; and you need long-term goals that you know will take some time but that are important enough to you that you're willing to keep working toward them.

Don't just think about these things, then sigh and doubt your ability to achieve them or, as can often happen, get distracted and forget all about them—*write your goals and timelines for achieving them on paper.* To become more effective in setting and pursuing these three categories of goals, devote a folder to each, listing the goals, the amounts of money needed, and your target dates for completion. If you're not sure when you can reach a given goal, come up with a target date range instead (for example, "two to three years from now" or "within the next ten to fifteen years").

It's not always fun to think about money or to do the hard work of planning how you can accomplish your financial goals. Hence you need all the help you can get. Buy good books on the subject, and use planning materials that inspire you—colorful or cute supplies from your office supply store, for example. This is not the time to use dreary, dull materials that make you never want to see them again!

Use your imagination to turn your financial goal setting into an enjoyable endeavor. You may want to spend a few leisurely hours going through old magazines, clipping photos that inspire you or represent the goals you've set, then taping or pasting them onto a poster board collage or on the cover of the folder dedicated to that category of goals.

Don't Say "Budget"!

Most people recoil from the word *budgeting* because it sounds to them like deprivation and having no fun. There are many books on budgeting, so I won't go into the specifics here (see the Recommended Reading section for some helpful resources on this topic). Nearly all personal finance articles and books use the word "budget," but I know from my own and others' experience that it's a downer psychologically and can actually prevent positive approaches to money management, savings, smart buying decisions, and so on. I'd like to offer you a different way of looking at the whole "sticking to a budget" idea that will be far more inspirational and helpful to you.

Eliminate the word *budget* from your mind altogether. While most books on finances, especially for single parents, use that word, I've found that it can be counterproductive. That is, you look at your income, then at your monthly expenses, notice an unpleasant result when the latter is subtracted from the former, and go into "ostrich syndrome" mode: if things are that bad, your subconscious mind reasons, let's never think about finances again. After all, the reasoning goes, you have to avoid depression and be a good mom, which you can't do if you're upset about the draconian budgeting it seems you must do.

But keeping your head in the sand when it comes to money will only cause you more stress long term and results in late charges, overdraft fees, and other costly unpleasantries. Trust me, I know what I'm talking about: like so many others, I've succumbed to the ostrich syndrome at times, thinking that if I really examined my financial situation, I'd become overwhelmed or lose hope, which could affect my mothering. This is where the way we talk to ourselves and the words we use can make all the difference between inertia and productivity.

You may want to mentally replace the word *budget* with words that are more positive. Experiment with your own phrases for taking charge of this important part of your life that sound more inspiring than the phrase we see and hear all the time and tend to associate with hard times: "make a budget and stick to it." To get yourself motivated, try on descriptions for monitoring money in/money out and your three savings goals (cushion, short-term, and long-term): for instance, "my financial system," "my financial well-being," "my money management project," or "my financial plan and future goals."

Once you've settled on the best wording and approach, invest in a calendar or appointment book that displays an entire month at a time and record the due dates for all your recurring bills for every month in the coming year, with "advance notice" notes a few days ahead of the deadlines. Computer calendars are a good supplement but probably not a safe substitute for paper calendars. Next, calculate your monthly income, bills, and other expenses such as gas and food. Then subtract the latter from the former to see how much "wiggle room" you have.

But don't panic if that number isn't a pleasant one! Instead, simply note the amount of extra money you'd need to more easily meet your expenses each month. Once you have a clear snapshot of your current financial situation, you can start looking into ways to trim expenses (such as dropping extra channels on your cable bill) and/or increase your income (such as finding a better-paying job). Refer to chapter 6, "Getting Organized," for ideas about organizing your financial paperwork—being organized and not constantly feeling that you're "missing something" is half the battle.

Be sure not to focus only on cutting back; one of my pet peeves about financial gurus is that they seldom mention the obvious fact that you may simply need to make more money! Once your mind has a clear goal such as increasing your income and you take steps to increase your confidence, you'll be amazed what you'll be able to accomplish. Too often we get stuck and discouraged by thinking only of what we can give up without equal emphasis on what we can gain with the right attitude, creativity, and persistence.

The point is to make money management and financial goal-setting less of a chore and more doable. However you choose to label and design your own system, make sure that it makes you feel willing, even eager (1) to tackle any current problems that need to be resolved, (2) to develop a savings and bill-paying system that's easy to maintain even when you're busy or tired, and (3) to set positive goals for your future.

As a single mom, you may have financial challenges, but don't let them overtake your life or your family life. Even if your cash flow problems are pressing, you can pray for God to guide you in finding ways of resolving them over time and to help you learn the healthy habit of "letting it go" emotionally once you've done all you can at the moment to manage and improve your finances for greater security and happiness in the future.

Your Job

Nobody but you can determine what kinds of jobs are likely to make you happy, content, or utterly miserable. This evaluation depends, in turn, on the phase of life you're in and how many of your practical, social, psychological, and spiritual needs are being met by your current job. Rather than being a simple matter of a job providing you with a sense of meaning and purpose or of promotion potential, for example, the most realistic appraisal of your job will take many factors into consideration. The degree to which your job or career is right for you has to do with how well it does or doesn't meet most of your needs.

In thinking about this important area of your life, it can be helpful to consider where you currently are on psychologist Abraham Maslow's famous hierarchy of needs. Let's go from the bottom level up, since this is how life really works: first things first. While you may have ideas for what you most want to be doing in the future, you first need to make sure that you have sufficient financial security before taking risks and expanding or changing your career. In other words, focusing on the top needs when the lower, most basic requirements aren't being met won't work.

Physiological and Safety Needs: Survival and Security

Many of us have been in dire straits at one time or another and have had to survive very difficult situations: totally broke, recovering from an addiction, coping with depression, feeling discouraged after lengthy unemployment, in serious debt, homeless, or victim-

> **The Bright Side of Single Mothering**
>
> You can design your own career and lifestyle more independently, without arguing or interference.

ized by domestic violence. At such times, our top priority is the health and safety of ourselves and our children. The saying "beggars can't be choosers" comes to mind here, and while it's not what we'd prefer, the idea behind the saying is valid: in some situations we can't be too picky. Nonetheless, we should remind ourselves that if we keep working toward a better future, we eventually *will* have more choices. When you're about to fall off a cliff, you'd better grab onto any branch or ledge you can reach. Forget having a sense of purpose, status, high salary, or promotion potential in a job: your first and foremost need is to survive.

The best job you can find during a very difficult phase of your life may not be much to brag about, but if it keeps you safe, it's serving its purpose. Because this kind of "safety job" is often low-wage or unpleasant (though some of them can be calming or fun), you'll probably move onto another job as soon as you can. Many single mothers need two of these jobs at the same time.

If you're in this boat, ask yourself if the job is at least keeping you and your children safe. If the answer is yes, you may find that it's best to stay put for the time being. If the answer is no, you're going to need to look for a better job, or supplement it with some other job or source of income, as soon as possible. To keep your spirits up, promise yourself that you'll make positive career changes in the not-too-distant future.

Most jobs in this category don't offer health insurance, and that's a real disadvantage—but remember, a safety job is the branch you're grabbing onto until you get stronger and more secure, and needn't last forever. Public assistance may become an issue here, and you shouldn't hesitate to apply for food stamps, low-cost hous-

"Homeless, Not Hopeless": Seeing the Tough Times as Temporary

A journalist once asked me how I was able to hold my head up during the period when my son and I were homeless. He wanted to know how I was able to overcome the shame. My fast response was—"Wait a minute. We were homeless, not hopeless."

He seemed surprised and couldn't understand how that was possible, even when I pointed out that our state of homelessness never defined who we were. My attitude at the time was that it was only a temporary condition, one that I was being given the opportunity to change as I became skilled in the field of my choice.

Chris Gardner, *Start Where You Are*[4]

ing, and other forms of financial assistance to get you through the hard times and on to a better situation. Additionally, most states now have health insurance programs such as SCHIP for children of lower income families, even those families that do not qualify for Medicaid. If you're interested in pursuing this for your children, contact your local social services agency or your governor's office for more information on the benefits that are available and how to apply for them.

I remember one time period when I was a grad student with two jobs that didn't pay much, and a friend urged me to apply for food stamps because my income was so low and I had a child depending on me. I finally went to apply, sat down in the waiting room of the "welfare" office, and panicked because of signs with the word "welfare" on the walls, the dingy atmosphere, the jaded clerks who took my name, and the long lines of women with children and babies. I quickly left in horror. In retrospect, that was pretty foolish, though I also understand that I, like so many others, had taken to heart the ridiculous things said by politicians at the time about "welfare queens." As a result of this internalization of contempt by others, I failed to get that little boost of financial help.

There's a lot of judgment when it comes to public assistance, but if you and your family really need it for a while, don't suffer due to fears of that judgment the way I did. Even at that time, I realized that this wasn't what anyone would prefer, but those women standing in line and waiting hours in those old chairs were showing a lot of courage just to persevere. And perseverance is what it's all about when you're struggling to provide for your children.

Esteem and Actualization Needs: Your Goals and Your Dreams

It's easy, as a single mother juggling multiple demands, to get so caught up in the must-do's that the want-to's take a backseat. Or, if neglected long enough, your aspirations may disappear altogether. More than likely, you have a job or even two that must be maintained to keep your family going with food on the table, clothes on their backs, and a roof over their heads. Next in line come the other needs of your children—for school supplies, medical care, and other necessities. The next priorities are usually your children's wants or the hopes you hold for their growth and development: music lessons, tutoring, sports equipment and fees, school trips, books, games . . . the list is endless. Last on the list—yes, the very last—are often your goals and dreams.

Perhaps the ideas you nurtured as a child are still there but constantly put on the back burner. This is understandable, because your priorities are focused on your children and their futures. You may enjoy your current job, and if this is so, count yourself fortunate indeed. Your career may be the one you chose long ago, and it may be going well. If this is the case, you may nonetheless have "extracurricular" goals that got lost in the shuffle: playing your favorite sport, taking art classes, traveling, taking dance lessons, or joining book clubs. While these interests may not seem important right now, they should not be delayed indefinitely, because they

> ### Reminding Yourself to Be Thankful, Even When You Want Something More
>
> Entrepreneur Sheila Brooks, who was raised in the ghetto, told me most of the kids she grew up with are dead, in jail, or still impoverished, but she "beat the odds" through hard work and unshakable faith in a Higher Power. "I truly believe that all things are possible with God. Every day I spend time in meditation and prayer. I thank my Higher Power for everything He has given me. When I do that, I know that no matter how bad things are, I can overcome."
>
> Barbara Stanny, *Secrets of Six-Figure Women*[5]

enrich your spirit, improve your motivation, and replenish you in ways you may have forgotten.

In many cases, however, single mothers end up feeling stuck in jobs that never were their first choice or, even if they once were, are now stressful, boring, or exhausting. Particularly if you became a single mother through circumstances that caught you off guard and for which you weren't prepared financially, you may have more or less stumbled into your current job or career. Time has a way of getting away from us when we're consumed with caring for others; months turn into years, and before long we find ourselves dreading the alarm clock because it means another day of unpleasant or overwhelming work. We may wonder, to quote the Talking Heads song, "Where *is* my beautiful life?"

David Allen, author and creator of the personal organization and strategy system entitled "Getting Things Done," notes that by focusing on the next action, you are telling yourself that change is possible and that you can do something to make it happen. This is far more powerful than simply repeating vague self-affirmations.

To this let me be a witness; I've tried just about everything, including the vague affirmations route that got me absolutely nowhere. If you, like me, are prone to the ostrich syndrome, it can magnify any overly optimistic thinking you may be in the habit of

using whenever money problems rear their ugly heads. Forget affirmations *unless* they're highly specific to you, the areas you want
to improve, the goals you're determined to achieve no matter what,
or antidotes tailored to changing your current thinking habits.

Plans go wrong for lack of advice; many counselors bring success.

Proverbs 15:22

I run straight to the goal with purpose in every step.

1 Corinthians 9:26

Work hard and cheerfully at whatever you do, as though you were working for the Lord rather than for people.

Colossians 3:23

Hope deferred makes the heart sick, but when dreams come true, there
is life and joy.

Proverbs 13:12

*Lord, help me to manage the challenges of my job and
to keep moving toward my dreams and goals with real-
ism combined with optimism and faith. I pray for your
wisdom, God, in handling our finances and providing
the best that I can for my children. Help me to remember
too that happy families may not have enough money,
but they can always have enough love. Amen.*

8

Restoring Your Faith
and Confidence

It's easy to feel confident and hopeful when things are going well. But when the going gets rough, when the stability we've worked so hard to create for our family seems to be slipping, those joyful qualities—faith, confidence, even that little spring in our step that says, "I can do it!"—become harder to hold on to. No matter how we feel as single mothers, we simply can't afford to mope around or let things slide for too long. Our children count on us to be strong for them, provide for them, and take care of them.

Yet we're only human. And we're certainly not immune to the problems that many married parents face every day. The difference is that we must face these problems and make decisions about how to resolve them on our own, all the while continuing to work and keep our household going. We don't have the luxury to quit our job and stay home with the kids while our partner is the provider, or to go back to school whenever we want. Nor can we philosophically say, as those without children can, "Oh well, I tried." We all face adversity at one time or another. When problems pile up, what's a single mother to do?

Years ago in Nashville, I worked with a dynamic single mother who'd brought joy to hundreds of children and their parents. After her unexpected divorce and the loss of her husband's income, Lana didn't complain—she got busy. With verve and style, she'd managed to provide for her family while building a reputation as the area's best children's party organizer. Lana was a vivacious, talented woman who'd triumphed over adversity to create a loving home for her family.

But on the day I met her, Lana's faith—in herself and in God—was at rock bottom.

Building Her Own Business

A small but lively forty-six-year-old woman with blonde hair and blue eyes, Lana had an easy smile and a contagious laugh. She told me how her party business began. "I just stumbled on it, to tell you the truth, after helping some friends give parties for their children. The kids begged for more!" Lana beamed with pride and satisfaction.

"I never had any training or anything. But I've always been a kid at heart, and I used to love giving theme parties for my kids with all the bells and whistles—clowns, magicians, jugglers, hayrides, the works. You see," she said, looking up at my office window, "my mother and I had a difficult relationship. But she always showed her love at birthdays and holidays by giving me these great parties, and I love seeing that joyful look on kids' faces when something magical happens at a party. Their parents really appreciate knowing that the party will be a success. *They've* built my business, really, just by word of mouth."

Falling Down

Most of us would consider Lana a smashing success as a single mother. She was determined to overcome her grief at losing her marriage, and she did. With the kind of energy, creativity, and daring that most of us only dream of, she'd single-handedly built a business that supported her and her children when they were small. As she told me how much she loved her work and how proud she was of her children, I wondered why she'd come to see me. Listening to her lively stories, I was waiting for the other shoe to drop.

"The parents always say, 'We love Lana and her parties!' See, I brought this article." She pulled a newspaper clipping out of her purse and thrust it toward me. The article, "Demand Overwhelms Supply at Local Party Business," featured a photo of children looking up in awe as a magician performed by candlelight. Suddenly I heard sobbing. I looked up to see Lana wiping tears away.

"It's been so wonderful. I have more business than I could ever want. *Right now* I have thirty-nine unanswered messages on my machine! But what can I tell those parents? I can't go on. For some mysterious reason, I'm bankrupt, and I'm just so tired and ashamed that I can't face anybody! What am I going to do?" She covered her face with her hands.

How could this woman possibly be broke? Was she a shopaholic? Did she let her success go to her head? Was she irresponsible, buying one frivolous item after another?

Not at all. Lana had made none of the usual mistakes that ruin people financially. And *that* was why she'd come to see me: she just couldn't understand what she'd done wrong and why she had more business than ever but couldn't even pay her mortgage. She also wondered why she was hiding the truth—not only from her loyal customers but from her children, parents, and friends as well. She'd also stopped praying, saying, "What's the point? God obviously isn't listening to me anymore."

Selling Herself Short

After several sessions of working through her feelings of failure and shame, Lana came in one day looking worn out but clear-eyed. She'd begun to realize where she had first gone wrong—a realization with both practical and spiritual implications.

All of Lana's misfortunes could be traced to this fundamental error: she had never charged enough for her services. The very enthusiasm and generosity that made her so popular with parents led her to give, and give, and give, without asking for anything more than the minimum costs to keep her bills paid.

Over the years, with rising business costs, increased property taxes, a car that finally gave out, and medical bills her HMO wouldn't cover, her expenses had escalated while her fees had not. She didn't want to disappoint those parents who raved about her talents and recommended her to all their friends. After a while, the balance sheet began to tilt toward the red, but she kept thinking that all she needed was more business.

But more business without higher fees only put her further behind. She began to cut corners to make ends meet. With a shudder, she described that fateful day when a clown she'd hired, for a lower fee than her usual performer would accept, showed up drunk. Fortunately, she'd been looking for him outside because he was late and intercepted him before the children could see him. Barely avoiding a real disaster, she was forced to improvise as a substitute for the clown. This was, not surprisingly, a disappointment for the children.

These snafus began to happen more frequently as Lana scrambled to make ends meet, doing more of the catering and entertaining herself to avoid hiring expensive professionals. She was increasingly stressed and exhausted, and she dreaded each new party. A few negative comments could now be heard, but Lana always managed to cover up—just barely. The dominoes were beginning to fall, one after another. Her business, on which her family and her own well-being depended, was coming undone.

Self-Reflection for Course Correction

Lana had made a very common single-mother mistake: in her efforts to "keep on keepin' on" so that her children wouldn't have to be uprooted, she had settled for less than she deserved and less than she needed for a stable future.

While that mistake may seem to have been the result of her desire to make the parties affordable, there's more to this story. Lana, like many single mothers, didn't so much devalue herself as much as she accepted the devaluation of society. True, she had some old issues with her mother, as so many of us do, but she knew her mother loved her and wanted her to succeed. And Lana had always felt confident about her abilities in school, where she was an excellent student.

After the divorce, she began to think—though not consciously—that she had been "dumped" and that therefore she should be happy with whatever she could get. On a more subtle level, after her husband left, for the first time she noticed her pastor's frequent sermons about the infamous "broken home" and the unworthy "fatherless home." This caused her great sadness and confusion: why was she being pitied and judged for what her *husband* had done?

For a time she tried to ignore it, but eventually the pastor's prejudices seeped into the congregation. She couldn't help but notice the disapproving looks from church elders and married couples. Hurt and angry, Lana decided to find a more welcoming church where her family would be embraced and respected. Like many single mothers, Lana was all too willing to blame herself for everything—her husband's affair, the divorce, and so on—but she wasn't about to let her children feel "less than."

We single mothers are famous for "buying high and selling low." As any stockbroker will tell you, this is the worst possible attitude for anyone who cares about their future. And who cares more about the future than we single mothers, who think of little else? Our children depend on us and *are*, in many ways, our future.

Twinkle, Twinkle, Little Star, How You Think Is How You Are

Are you an optimist, a pessimist, or a realist? Chances are, you're a blend of all three. You may be an optimist about life in general but a pessimist about money. You may be a realist regarding your current situation but an optimist about your future. Or you may feel optimistic about your children's futures or the way *other* people's lives are going but pessimistic about your own. Becoming aware of the way you tend to think about yourself, your abilities, your past, and your future is the first step in charting a new course for yourself and your family.

If you honestly reflect on the successful and not-so-successful decisions that you've made in the past (including those instances when you've avoided making a decision—thus making a decision by default), you can change course. But first you must discover and deal with assumptions that may have caused you to "settle" or otherwise fail to live up to your potential.

Self-Reflection: Your First Step toward a Better Life

> And the day came when the risk to remain tight in the bud was more painful than the risk it took to blossom.
>
> Anaïs Nin

Reflecting on your past when trouble hits can feel threatening—especially when you're a single mother who feels she must be strong (i.e., perfect) at all times. But the costs of protecting yourself from change or from uncomfortable facts will eventually outweigh the false security you get from hiding your head in the sand. Reflecting on your past decisions and emotional reactions (what happened *in* you) as well as external events (what happened *to* you) is absolutely necessary when problems start popping up. To maintain your family's stability and your own happiness, commit yourself to begin a new habit: the "winner's two-step" of (1) *self-reflection*, then (2) *course correction*.

Before you can do either, however, you'll want to make sure that you can really think for yourself. It's so easy to think with our emotions, or to accept popular opinion, or to think only "inside the box." Ask yourself the following questions, and notice those areas in which you've made decisions that may have seemed okay at the time but, in retrospect, weren't in keeping with your true priorities.

Have You Been Led *by Your Emotions?*

When essential aspects of a single mother's life (child care, job, car, housing) break down, trouble isn't far behind. Because we have no partner to fall back on, we tend to panic first and think later. This can lead to all sorts of bad decisions or even paralysis—"deer in the headlights" syndrome. When that check doesn't arrive, or we lose our job, we may be so frightened that we fail to act at all. We may be so overwhelmed by emotion that our rational minds don't have a chance to guide us. We may sit there scanning the job ads with fear and dread, doubting our ability to get an interview or to produce a decent résumé.

Have You Been Limited *by Your Situation?*

A single mother's confidence usually doesn't deteriorate rapidly; it's a more subtle process, one that begins with those sympathetic looks that strangers give us. We begin, after a while, to see ourselves the same way—as someone who needs sympathy and is "less than" married women, particularly wealthier women. Without realizing it, we begin to see ourselves as lucky just to keep our children with us, or to have health insurance for the family, or to have a roof over our heads. If the child support comes in on time, or if we can just keep our jobs, we "lie low" and try to be satisfied with conditions that may or may not be acceptable to us.

Fear-Based Contentment vs. the Real Thing

There's nothing wrong with contentment—contentment is what most people seek. What can lead to serious problems in the future is fear-based contentment, a sort of "batten down the hatches" mentality that comes from believing we're not worth more. Our contentment, like Lana's, is fear-based when it prevents us from asking for what we really need not just to survive (a perilous foundation for any family) but to *thrive*. Every single mother's situation is different—we have different talents, weaknesses, educational degrees, economic backgrounds, and life experiences—but God desires that we, like married parents, live abundantly.

Even if we struggle financially all our lives, we will be far happier if we acknowledge that God wishes the best for all of us. In a sometimes brutal and unjust world it is comforting for us, and important for our children psychologically and spiritually, to remember that in God's eyes, our families deserve the very same resources and care as any other. Real contentment comes from knowing that God *wants* you to be confident and proactive, even when you're hitting the road bumps and potholes of life. This means that when you feel yourself stumbling or falling, you will

- pray for the strength to face those problems you've ignored or avoided;
- expect God to gently help you recognize past errors or wrong turns;
- begin taking steps to correct your course;
- believe in yourself even when other people criticize or blame you;
- ask God to renew your faith and your confidence along the way;

- give thanks for even the slightest improvements in your attitude, your actions, and your family life.

Course Correction: Your Second Step for a Better Life

Once she saw the light, Lana decided to make things right. Looking back on that series of mistakes was tough, but once she understood how she'd gone wrong, her single-mother spirit kicked into gear. After all, she was a survivor—but now she wanted something more. She decided to thrive.

"I was trying too hard to be 'nice,'" Lana said one day, looking well put together in a tailored dress and heels, "when what I really needed was to value myself and my family as highly as any *married* parent would by asking—no, insisting!—on the fees that I needed to maintain a profitable business. But that was the problem, I guess—I didn't really feel I deserved that."

Lana looked out the window and paused. I was impressed by her self-discovery. "My success seemed like such a fluke—I was always terrified that people would say, 'Sorry, you're *not worth* more.' I was still trying to win everyone's love, so I couldn't stand up for myself. I guess I did feel second rate: now I was a single mother who'd been 'dumped' by her husband, and after all those things the preacher said about single-mother homes and the distance, or pity, or whatever it was that I sensed from the congregation, *deep down, I thought that God had rejected me too.*"

Her first step toward stability was to come clean with her customers, friends, parents, and—hardest of all—children. She used prayer and therapy during this emotionally demanding process: she would pray for the strength to be honest, then admit her financial dilemma to a customer or family member, and then release her feelings of sorrow, embarrassment, shame, and loss in the safety of the therapy room.

The Bright Side of Single Mothering

Your child will learn to adapt well to the personality and communication style differences of authority figures. If your child has extensive playdates and sleepovers as part of a child care exchange, he or she is thus supervised by different parents with different styles. Children who regularly have these experiences often grow up to be more confident socially with a wide array of people than kids who don't.

Next on her agenda was consulting with a bankruptcy lawyer because the bank was about to foreclose on the house—the only home her children had ever known. But that's not all. Lana had used her personal credit cards to pay for materials and performers that she could no longer afford during the last six years of her business. She'd also borrowed money from friends and associates, who never hesitated to lend the funds because they knew her business was booming (on the surface, that is).

This was a very hard time for Lana, but she was beginning to truly respect herself, including her talents *and* her vulnerabilities, for the first time. "At my age, or maybe it's just because of what I've been through this year, I just don't have what it takes to run my own business. Maybe one day I will, but not now. I'm going to apply for temp jobs and try to find steady employment. I know I have these 'great talents,' as everybody keeps telling me—but right now what I most need is rest, recovery, and a stable, *sufficient* income."

Working with the lawyer, she came up with a plan to discharge her credit card debt, and she promised her friends that she would eventually pay them back in full, with interest. With great trepidation, she placed an ad in the newspaper for a roommate to help her pay the mortgage. This came as a jolt to her children, but when they saw how much calmer their mother was becoming, they tried to adjust to the idea. After many interviews, Lana finally met a hardworking grad student who was grateful for that spare bedroom.

Lana was relieved when the kids finally accepted the situation and realized its necessity.

The Courage to Ask for What You Need

I've always admired the kind of courage that Lana exhibited in the face of, as Stephen Covey puts it, "*dis*couraging" people and circumstances. We talk a lot in our culture about heroism, as if the only heroic deed is that which risks life and limb. But what about psychological and spiritual heroism? Admitting our mistakes and correcting our course, knowing that others may misunderstand, criticize, or condemn us for our past mistakes—*that* takes real courage too.

For some it also takes courage to admit, let alone to ask for, what they need. Even when we're talking with God, we may be reluctant to ask for the same level of help, care, and well-being that others (who seem to us more "worthy") seek. But that is not what Jesus taught. We are to come to God as children to a parent, asking with confidence for what we need. Even if circumstances prevent us from achieving all that we would like, we will certainly find greater strength and calm if we ask, seek, and knock with the assurance that God stands ready to help and guide us.

Through self-reflection and course-correction, Lana got her life back on track. Two years later, I ran into Lana again. She'd gotten a few temp jobs, one of which turned into a permanent job with a higher salary. Relieved of the constant strain of trying to keep the business afloat, she began to realize that she'd been lonely for years! She tentatively began to date ("I was so rusty!" she laughed) and to nurture friendships with women at her church. She'd also begun taking yoga, traveling, and giving art classes for children on Saturdays. Because Lana asked God for what she needed and then took action, her life had become more balanced and joyful, her children felt more secure, and her faith had been renewed.

Restore Your Faith and Your Confidence

Do you regularly stop to reflect and, if necessary, correct your course? If you're like many people, you may skip this vital process because you're busy or because self-examination makes you anxious. As a single mother, you may want to provide a "house on a rock" for your children yet fear having to admit to yourself, or to God, when things seem to be going wrong or your confidence is flagging.

Neither optimists nor pessimists are comfortable with self-reflection, but for opposite reasons: the optimist doesn't want to see anything bad (because that means everything *isn't* rosy), and the pessimist is scared to death that she'll see something good (hence her gloomy forecasts are wrong)!

Only clear-eyed realists who are willing to see the positive *and* the negative can assess where they are, where they've been, and where they want to go. Avoiding the extremes of optimism or pessimism, think about your life for a moment. What's going well, and what isn't? Think about those aspects of your life that are causing you the most concern, frustration, or self-doubt, then list them here. Next to each, write "Self-Reflect" if you're not sure what's behind the problem or how to remedy it and "Course Correct" if you are.

Areas of Concern	Self-Reflect/Course Correct
1.	
2.	
3.	
4.	
5.	
6.	
7.	
8.	
9.	
10.	

Next, make a date with yourself to attend to each of these areas, and write the time and date next to each item. Plan steps to resolve the problem or to reflect on what might have led to it. Even if a problem is beyond your control, schedule a time for self-reflection. You may need to alter your attitude toward it or to change the role and/or importance that this difficulty has been playing in your life.

If something comes up that interferes with your date to self-reflect or course correct, be sure to reschedule; for goodness' sakes, don't stand yourself up! Stay the course, and if you need emotional support or practical guidance, find a way to get it. Attend to each of these items, one step at a time. Reward yourself for every effort in the right direction. If you're not sure you've got what it takes, ask a friend or therapist to help you get started. And above all, remember: there is Someone watching over you, just waiting for you to ask for the courage, the help, and the wisdom you need.

He lifted me out of the pit of despair, out of the mud and the mire.

Psalm 40:2

Come to me, all of you who are weary and carry heavy burdens, and I will give you rest.

Matthew 11:28

For I have given rest to the weary and joy to the sorrowing.

Jeremiah 31:25

What is faith? It is the confident assurance that what we hope for is going to happen. It is the evidence of things we cannot yet see.

Hebrews 11:1

Now and then I forget to believe in myself, even when I believe in you, God. When this happens, I get confused and stop advocating for myself and my children; my

119

*dreams seem too difficult to achieve, and I feel like giv-
ing up. I pray that when this happens, you'll reassure me
that I can do what needs to be done. With your words
and love, please lift me up, give me new strength, and
help me to fly again as on the wings of eagles. Amen.*

9

Taking Care of Your Child

No matter who you are or what your life is like, as a parent you're practically programmed to do all you can to help your child be happy and successful. There's just something in parents that makes us highly dedicated to this goal. I've seen many mothers who are in the depths of depression or anxiety suddenly stop crying and say, "The other thing is, I'm so worried about my daughter's grades . . ." or "My son doesn't have many friends, he's so lonely—how can I help him?"

It's pretty remarkable the way we can put ourselves second when we sense that our child needs help or support. We single mothers feel especially concerned about our children because we know that we are our child's biggest or sole active advocate.

We're usually very effective in advocating for our child when the signs of trouble are obvious. A child who comes crying to you, saying that he's sad about the death of a pet, is communicating clearly what is needed: empathetic listening and guidance to help him adjust to the loss.

What's tougher to "diagnose" and respond to effectively is a subtle signal that may or may not reflect a deeper problem that requires extra help. For instance, your child's emotional changes *could* be the result of typical teenage moodiness, *or* they could indicate more serious sadness or anxiety.

Katie, a thirty-nine-year-old mother of two, noticed some changes in her thirteen-year-old daughter Kaitlin: staying in her room with the door closed, greater irritability, and a sudden change in friends. Katie tried to get her daughter to tell her what was wrong, but Kaitlin always said, "Nothing," went back in her room, and slammed the door. Unsure if she was being too intrusive *or* not inquisitive enough, Katie asked if she should pursue the problem or let it go to see if Kaitlin would in time return to her old self.

This is an example of the classic dilemma—whether one should insist on addressing concerns or back off with a wait-and-see approach—that all parents face sooner or later. Single mothers have the added challenge of trying to assess without a partner's input how serious the problem is. As Katie and I discussed the changes she was worried about, it became clear that Kaitlin's recent isolating behaviors and marked mood changes, particularly when combined with a change in friends, were indeed concerning.

Not having family nearby, Katie had only her own observations to guide her at this point. When she asked Kaitlin's teachers if they'd noticed changes, they answered that she was still doing well in class and that they hadn't observed emotional changes. Katie's decision to wait and see for a short time made sense, but she was wise to realize, when the problems persisted and at times seemed worse, that it was risky to try to address them on her own.

Katie called her pediatrician about these changes. The doctor advised her to make sure there was nothing more serious brewing by taking Kaitlin to see a mental health professional. If, after an evaluation, the clinician and Katie agreed that these changes were normal adolescent moodiness, Katie could relax and work toward improving communication with Kaitlin. If, on the other hand, deeper issues surfaced during the evaluation, Katie would certainly feel concerned but would also feel relief from knowing she'd been, as a responsible and loving parent, providing her child with needed care.

It can be challenging to insist on getting help for an older child or teen when we're unsure how to proceed. As single mothers, we're often hesitant to be the "bad guy" or otherwise make our child angry at us. Though Katie did hesitate at first when Kaitlin angrily announced that she didn't want to see a therapist, she persevered, insisting calmly that Kaitlin go "at least one time, just to see what the doctor thinks."

As it turned out, the therapist determined that Kaitlin was feeling quite depressed and rejected due to peer conflicts at her school and that she was developing an eating disorder in an attempt to cope with the anxiety she was feeling. After the evaluation, Katie was amazed when, after all her initial resistance to talking with a mental health professional, Kaitlin asked to see the therapist again (asking to continue in therapy is actually quite common when a child or teen has been privately suffering emotionally). After the second session, Kaitlin opened up to her mom, admitting that she'd been extremely depressed for months and had been purging after meals, both as an "anxiety reliever" and as a method to become as thin as the "popular" girls.

Concerns about Your Child

Some parents have it easy—they don't have concerns about their children for quite a few years. But nobody has a free ride—into every childhood and into every parenthood, a few raindrops will eventually fall. When a child has problems, whether minor or major, having a partner can make life easier (that is, *if* one's partner has good insight and emotional balance). Discussing such concerns and trading off responsibilities when one parent gets tired or over-wrought can be very helpful.

Even those couples who normally don't get along very well some-how manage to cooperate when they're sufficiently worried about their child. If you and your children's father can work together when they encounter a problem, and if you trust his judgment, by all means make use of this resource. Most dads, no matter how conflicted or distant they've been with their ex-partners, are still very concerned about their children.

However, if there are significant problems that make you leery of getting your child's father involved, it may be best to proceed with the help of other relatives, friends, and/or professionals as the need arises.

Consider your responses to the inventory at the beginning of this book. Did you note areas in your child's life that require your attention or that call for improvement? If so, list them on a piece of paper that you can put in a file folder labeled with your child's name. You may, for example, have concerns about your child's schoolwork. Or you may be worried about issues such as your child's conflicts with friends, unusual fatigue, or low self-esteem.

Whatever your concern, list it in your child's folder with a *next action step* written beside it. In other words, don't just list concerns such as "Gaining a lot of weight" or "Distractible," but add the all-important next steps, such as "Call pediatrician tomorrow re: Melissa's weight gain" or "Ask Mom if she thinks Jeff has seemed more distractible and hyper lately." Or it may be "Call the school tomorrow to ask about an evaluation for learning disabilities" or

> Jesus had to actively shepherd his disciples through good times and bad. He was there for them, whether they were tired, angry, frightened, or sad. We who seek to raise our children as Jesus would must be there for them, whether they're making our day or breaking our heart.
>
> Teresa Whitehurst, *How Would Jesus Raise Your Child?*[1]

"Make an appointment with his teacher to discuss his homework load." These next actions should be doable so that you can start addressing the problem tomorrow, even if the first step is just a quick phone call. You can begin to check off the areas of concern, one by one, as you address them.

Keeping a separate folder on each of your children is an effective strategy to keep track of medical and school records, birth certificates, and similar forms in one place (if there are numerous records per child, make a separate folder labeled as [Your Child's Name]: Records File). On the top page in the folder, note any concerns you may have, along with the next action to address them. Keeping track of your concerns, as well as your child's important records, is far better than worrying, then rushing the kids to school and yourself to work, coming home and doing your nightly routines, and never fully addressing and resolving the concern you had about your child.

Creating a folder for each child is a loving step, and though it takes a few minutes to gather all the records in one place, this strategy will save you lots of time and emotional energy because it can help you get into the habit of reviewing your folders each week or so to stay ahead of the game. It's a great way to feel confident that you're taking care of your children and addressing their needs no matter how busy your life becomes.

Physical/Health Section

The obvious signs of illness or injury are not at issue here: most mothers have learned the ropes about fevers, congestion, sore throats, earaches, the signs of common childhood diseases, bruises, cuts and broken bones. Unless you're a new mother—and having your first baby is a learning experience regarding which symptoms require which steps—you already know how to take care of your child's health, when to call the doctor, and so on. Nutrition, exercise, and sleep are likewise familiar issues for most parents. There are many books and magazine articles to guide you, not to mention internet sources of information.

What bears noting is that more subtle factors can slip off our radar when we're busy, or if we assume that our child is experiencing emotional problems when in fact there are actually physiological issues going on. While it's beyond the scope of this book to cover all the bases on this subject, here's a sampling of the kinds of problems that may resolve on their own; they may, on the other hand, appear psychological—and this may be the case. Whether the problem originates with body, mind, or spirit, a wise mother will monitor the situation and call the doctor if symptoms and other changes persist or worsen over time:

- Persistent fatigue; complaining of being "tired" all the time
- Frequent moderate-to-severe headaches
- Dizziness, visual changes (aside from typical needs for glasses) or new clumsiness/lack of coordination
- Brief "zoning out" episodes
- Soreness or pain anywhere in the body, from an injury or an unknown origin, that continues for too long or seems to get worse
- Severe, disabling menstrual periods
- Constant bad breath, even when teeth have been brushed
- Asking "What'd you say?" more frequently and needing TV or stereo volume higher than previously

Remember, you are your child's best advocate, so trust your instincts when something seems amiss with his or her health. Even if you think you're being a worrywart (always a possibility when you're a loving parent), it pays to call your physician just in case to make sure the sudden changes or prolonged symptoms/complaints you've noticed aren't cause for concern. Keep in mind that you may need to speak up or seek a second opinion if you're told there's no problem yet your child remains sick or in pain.

Dr. Jerome Groopman, author and Harvard physician, has written that even parents who are physicians can encounter trouble because some health care professionals assume that doctors "know too much" and are thus likely to imagine their child has every symptom they learned about in medical school. Dr. Groopman recommends that parents ask all the questions they need to ask, provide the information they feel the doctors and nurses should be aware of, and express any doubts they have about the diagnosis or treatment—even if this means they'll irritate the medical staff or even have to change doctors. Dr. Groopman should know: his own child was misdiagnosed as a baby and turned out to have an illness that could have been fatal had Dr. Groopman not questioned the treating doctor's judgment.[2]

In using the following two sections of your folder, simply make notes for your own use. Note the date, then record what had just happened that might have triggered the statements, attitude, or behavior you're concerned about (for example, a sibling grabbing his toy or game; an overly delayed meal; becoming too tired or overstimulated at a party; walking by a group of kids who tease or reject her). Also note the context (situation or circumstances) in which the comments or behavior occurred (at home, at school, in the car, at a particular friend's house, or while rushing to catch the bus). Like a child therapist or a schoolteacher, you'll be staying one step ahead of the game by keeping similar records in order to see if a problem is fleeting, a once or twice only occurrence, or becoming a trend over time. Your goal is to let the little problems come and go without worrying about them but to be alert to *patterns*.

If, after referring to your folder a week or two later, you notice that problem areas have continued at the same level or even increased, you'll know that it's time to talk about the issue with your child, or you can ask a relative to talk with your child if they have

Realize the power of your child's friendships with other adults. Children can gain great comfort by confiding in adults other than their parents whom they like and trust. Aunts, uncles, and grandparents often enjoy listening to a child and are less likely to judge, overreact, or punish.

Gail Reichlin and Caroline Winkler, *The Pocket Parent*[3]

good rapport. See if you can start to understand why the problem is occurring, then read relevant books or ask friends, trusted relatives, or a counselor about the best way to address the problem.

If your child just won't open up to anyone and the problem continues to occur, it may be time to make an appointment with a counselor or doctor for an evaluation.

Psychological/Behavioral Section

Your child's cognitive abilities, psychological health, and social skills are other areas that you, as a mom, automatically monitor. You notice and feel concern, even if you're not sure what (if any) next steps to take in order to help, if your child:

1. Has difficulty understanding what the teacher wants (make sure there is not a hearing issue and that she can see the board); how to do the assigned homework; how to remember which materials to bring home when for projects; or how to organize his desk or make sense of his school papers once he gets home. This concern is especially important when the child does seem to be trying his hardest to remember and to get organized; some children need to be taught basic organizing skills, and in other cases there may be some subtle cognitive delays.

2. Obsesses on one aspect of a situation, an assignment, or even a playdate to the point where she's in her own little world, not interacting much with the other kids, or can't seem to

finish homework or chores because she's so fixated on one or more details and fails to see the "big picture." This can be related to a tendency toward obsessive-compulsive thinking/behavior, or to what's referred to as a high-functioning autism-spectrum disorder or a sensory processing disorder. All of these issues can be addressed and improved upon, given the right supports and techniques. There are many excellent books on the subject now, along with helpful support groups on these disorders all around the world.

3. Gets in frequent prolonged fights, verbal showdowns, or arguments with teachers, other children/teens, or parents. Such behavior may be followed by the "silent treatment" or an undercurrent of resentment for days after the incident. If left untreated, this kind of "prickly" hypersensitivity tends to increase rather than decrease as the child gets older. The underlying feelings as well as the habitual oppositional responses to conflicts or limits should be addressed through counseling and through parental consultations with the child's counselor, or through psychoeducational groups. It's best to catch this early because such psychological/behavioral habits can lead to rejection by others and lowered self-esteem in the child, who eventually notices that he can't control his emotions when angry.

4. Becomes exceedingly anxious before going to school ("school phobis," a panicky reaction related to fears/anxieties about the classroom or playground situation that he can't or won't talk about) or when any changes are made to his routine, his room, your schedule, or even the position of his toys on the shelf or silverware on the dinner table (obsessive-compulsive tendencies, a coping style developed when children have been chronically anxious).

5. Exhibits sadness, withdraws from others, stays in his room, does not respond to you or other adults beyond the minimal

words required, has a change in friends, exhibits isolating behavior with a sharp spike in the number of hours "losing herself" online, watching TV, or playing video games. Some children, particularly early adolescents, will actually cry and openly say they're depressed—but most will try to escape the feelings by withdrawing as described. In some cases, the sadness or clinically significant depression is coped with through distraction: by constantly hanging out with friends and staying as busy as possible. This "never stop or be alone" behavior is usually combined with an obvious preference not to be at home or to do anything quietly that could allow them to reflect and think and feel. This form of expressing depression is often associated with drug or alcohol use "socially" with friends who may be using substances recreationally—but for the depressed child it is a form of self-medication.

Every child goes through phases and changes over time. When should you become concerned, make notes in the section, and consider taking action yourself or with outside help?

If your child seems anxious, depressed, lonely, or angry *most of the time*, don't brush it off as "just his temperament" or "typical kid stuff." Certainly all children and teens have moods, but if there's one predominant emotion or a general moodiness that worries you, it's wise to look further into the matter.

If your child shows signs of cognitive delay and has a great deal of trouble organizing homework, her desk, her room, or her time—even if she's very smart in certain subjects—have her evaluated. If your child has a learning disability, an attention and/or hyperactivity problem, or a sensory processing deficit, it's better to know this now so that you can get your child the needed help and learn how to assist her in compensating for her weaker areas. When parents don't want to see such problems (which is very common), they tend to just push the child to try harder. Trying harder works when children do not have cognitive or sensory deficits impacting performance—but when they do, trying harder just creates more anxiety and tension and can lead to lower self-esteem when the extra effort, exerted day after day but with no new skills or compensatory techniques, doesn't pay off.

How can you handle any problem areas that seem to be persistent?

You can first try talking with your child. Many parents are amazed to hear their children open up with all sorts of explanations when they're with therapists but don't realize that if they as mom or dad offer some gentle wording and honest questions in a quiet environment (with no other siblings present or chaos going on in the background), they too can elicit important revelations.

For example, you can say, "You seem angry with your friends a lot lately—is something wrong?" or "I'm concerned because you seem kind of sad and don't want to go to school anymore—what's going on? Is it something about the kids at school, or is it something else?" Sometimes this is all it takes. You may learn that someone has been bullying your child or that he or she is experiencing some depression or anxiety due to internal worries or social anxiety related to not "fitting in" at school.

If your best efforts don't work, however, it's time to seek professional help. Call your child's doctor to talk about your concerns, or call a mental health center in your area to schedule an appointment for an evaluation. I've done many evaluations for children and teens that helped mom or dad understand *why* there's been a school phobia, or a quick temper, or a tendency to hang with the wrong kids, or a lonely withdrawal into video games. Quite often, you can take it from there with the help of a consultation or two regarding the child's specific needs and how you can assist your child.

At other times, a child may need a professional counselor to talk with for a number of sessions. This can be a real help to the parent, and single parents especially should take advantage of this whenever they feel there's a need. The following are some signs that your child may need this kind of professional help, at least for a while:

1. Declining school performance, coupled with expressions of apathy and helplessness.
2. The recent loss of a loved one, particularly someone in the family.
3. An abrupt change in behavior, ranging from some degree of hyperactivity to social isolation.
4. A marked change in sleeping or eating habits.
5. Familial disruptions, such as divorce, or other traumatic changes within the home.
6. Evidence that the teenager is being disparaged in the home.
7. An absence of normal social contacts.
8. Impulsiveness.[4]

When there's been a problem, it's important to pay attention. It may just be a passing phase, but if you use your mother's intuition, you'll know when this is something that you and your child can work out together and when it's time to consult with a professional. You'll feel more secure when you know that you have more than just your own perspective, if ever there's an issue that concerns you. Psychological and spiritual problems are often intertwined, and they're most troublesome when they've become a trend rather than isolated incidents here and there.

While you're at it, make note of those times when your child shows an increased level of empathy for a friend or sibling, is especially helpful around the house, or gives extra effort on a test or school project. Keep your child's drawings, and note the nice things that other people have said about your child's temperament, behavior, or kindness toward others. Every child has tantrums or seems difficult from time to time, and some children can even become rather hardened to pleas for help from peers, from siblings, or from mom. Thus it's especially important to keep track of the good things, the "happy accidents," and the personal and spiritual gifts that might otherwise go unnoticed.

Spiritual Section

Your child's spiritual development is both separate from and tied to his or her psychological and emotional development. It's separate because this is where faith comes in, which for children is closely tied to the feeling of being cherished and loved by God. The spiritual development of your child is related to confidence (versus doubt) that he or she is favored and valued by God. Every child wants to feel that he or she has unique gifts and a purpose in life. This confidence ebbs and flows depending on what's happening in our lives ("good luck" vs. "bad luck"; good grades vs. an unexpected F; feeling a part of the group vs. suddenly being teased by the popular kids, etc.). But your child's "set point"—the *usual* level of confidence or doubt that God cares and values him or her—is what you'll want to notice over time.

Some children have had cognitive or physical problems, some have had difficulty "fitting in" socially with peers, and others have suffered family losses, distressing conflicts in the family, or ongoing emotional difficulties. In any of these cases, the child's spiritual development may suffer because in childhood the tendency is to assume, "If I'm having these problems, it's because

---

The Bright Side of Single Mothering

Even if your children's father discouraged religion or spirituality, your faith and beliefs will provide your children with a positive perspective and foundation.

I'm bad, and if I'm bad, God doesn't love me as much as other kids."

It's a good idea to ask your child, in the right situation and at the right time, how he or she feels about God. If you sense confidence that God loves him or her no matter what, that's a very good sign. If your child expresses doubt that he or she is special to God, a sense that God has forgotten about him or her or never even cared, don't try to fix the problem then and there. Just listen openly without arguing or adding to the problem by showing how upset this makes you feel. Resolve to *later* note it in the spiritual section of your child's folder and to plan your next step for addressing the problem. Excellent next steps include:

1. Going to your local or online bookstore to find a good book on spiritual development in children. You may wish to ask a friend or someone at church for a good book on this topic.
2. Making an appointment to talk with your child's guidance counselor to ask what he or she has observed in your child.
3. Speaking with your child's youth minister or, if you don't have one at this time, with the minister of your church. If you prefer, you can ask a friend whose child has a great youth minister if she might connect you with that person.
4. Reassure your child every now and then regarding his or her special gifts, God's wish for them to find and develop their true talents and have a happy life, or whatever the issue is with your child. Note that with children and teens, the "now and then" schedule is what works best. Reassurance or encouragement provided too intensely or too often is usually discounted and is thus ineffective; it can even backfire when the child begins to wonder why you're constantly telling him how much God loves him or how special she is, thinking

something along the lines of, "Wow, I must be a real loser if my mom has to keep telling me I'm not!"

Yes, hearing that your child feels "un-special" or passed over can be painful to hear as a mom, but it's far better to know than to simply hope for the best, trying to believe that your child's spirit is okay (which we moms tend to do because we assume they *must know* how much they are cherished and talented). One mother told me that she felt shocked and sorrowful when her thirteen-year-old son said, "I don't have *any* talents. I'm not special in *any* way— nothing in school and nothing after school. There's nothing terrible *or* good about me—I'm just a nobody." While this does signal a common early-adolescence form of depression, it also speaks to the spiritual dimension: this boy believed in God and was raised in a religious environment, but over the years the strain of trying to find some way to shine in his competitive school had finally taken a toll on his spirit. He felt that he was a nobody, that he had nothing to offer, and that God wasn't too interested in him. As is often the case, this boy was actually quite bright and had been teased as a "nerd" by other kids as a result.

Spiritual faith is thus closely tied to the psychological realm in that a child who's depressed or angry or anxious is unlikely to be able to experience that sense of being special or treasured. Children need help when they are distressed. They need comforting and reas-

---

When a child stands out in some way—because he or she is different in terms of body size, learning abilities, clothing, religion, or race—a feeling of being "emotionally naked," too exposed to the world, is common. Parents can help by listening to the child's concerns and talking about his or her special strengths or talents. Every child is unique, valuable, and cherished by God, no matter what others may say, and it's up to us as parents to clothe them with this reassurance.

Teresa Whitehurst, *How Would Jesus Raise Your Child?*[5]

surance before they can feel truly valued. If your child or teenager seems unhappy, do all that you can to address this first.

Another aspect of spiritual development in children has to do with the way they treat others. While this is, once again, closely tied to psychological/emotional development, there are some ways in which the child's "default" view of other people, particularly parents, siblings, and peers, can become problematic at the spiritual level.

Even children who've been attending religious services all their lives can develop an antagonistic, defensive, non-empathetic, or pessimistic view of other people if (1) the religious training they've received emphasizes a punitive God just looking for mistakes to punish and a stark all-good/all-bad dichotomy between people, and/ or (2) he or she has frequently experienced physical punishments and loud expressions of anger in the home. Other factors that can lead to an anxious, easily-angered spirit in children include intense sibling rivalry (the feeling of having been "demoted" in a parent's eyes), a depressed or emotionally unavailable parent, and teasing or rejection by other children over a long period of time. Often several of these factors are combined and work together to counteract even the most intensive teachings about "turning the other cheek" or "treating others as you would have them treat you."

How should you handle this? Few children can or will articulate their distrust of other people, their tendency to want revenge whenever they feel slighted, or their view of God as a punishing parental figure to whom it thus makes no sense to pray. When you see these issues in your child, be an observer before you talk to or reassure him or her. Just record your concerns and, as time passes, note what the trigger for the attitude or behavior may have been (for example, being overly hungry or tired, witnessing a hostile argument between friends or siblings, or feeling overwhelmed with school or home chores). If you see a pattern of rigid defensiveness or vengefulness rather than an infrequent "meltdown," take the

None of the things that parents can do to make the soil good can be done all at once. They require time and patience. As a Chinese proverb says, "We don't have enough time to hurry." You can't force a seed to grow any faster. As I have learned from many a failed gardening project, fiddling with the seed or adding too much fertilizer and water causes the seedling to wither. All that concern was not good for it. Parents must do their best and let God do the rest.

You may know the story of the bamboo plant. It must receive nutrients and water for six years while it hibernates in the ground. Only in the sixth year does it grow visibly—but when it does, it reaches five feet or more in just a few months! So it is with Jesus' teachings. We may not see the fruit of them in our child for several years. This means that we must persevere in being there for our children, trusting that our gentle and loving attitude toward them is having an effect, whether or not we see visible results.

Nobody can mandate spiritual growth. We aren't God. We're just parents who care. For those who dare to strive toward parenting as Jesus would, helping children grow spiritually is more like being a gardener than a professor. The goal is to *prepare the soil* in which Jesus' teachings can take root and grow.

Teresa Whitehurst, *How Would Jesus Raise Your Child?*[6]

steps described above. And if the problem is impacting your child's ability to function at school, socially, or within the family, do make an appointment with a mental health professional. Later on, you'll be glad you did—and believe it or not, your child will probably thank you for doing so.

Helpful versus Unhelpful Guilt and Worry

As parents we all, sooner or later, feel guilty and worried. These may seem to be separate emotions, and in a sense they are, but for those of us who are single mothers, guilt over past mistakes or for having failed our child in some way tends to rotate in a vicious cycle, leading us to worry about the consequences of our mistakes, which then leads to even more guilt. Sometimes we assume that *because* we're single mothers, or have made choices we later regretted, or missed early signs of trouble:

1. we're bad mothers,
2. our child is ruined forever, and
3. we therefore should suffer guilt without end.

This kind of guilt and worry is unhelpful and counterproductive, and it can result in our getting so consumed with past mistakes that we fail to notice or effectively respond to current needs.

Sometimes, however, our parenting is improved when we heed new inklings of guilt or worry. Maybe our child's social anxieties *are* becoming disabling. Maybe we *did* fail to listen at dinner when our daughter was hinting that her grades were slipping and that a teacher disliked her. Maybe we *did* downplay the situation when our son told us he was being bullied at school. Maybe we *did* snap at our children for weeks on end after coming home stressed and exhausted from that awful job we should have quit a long time ago.

Or maybe, on even little matters, our own disorganization suddenly becomes apparent to us, such as when we notice that our child is the only student rushing to the school bus with wrinkled clothes and uncombed hair (one mother reported with chagrin that she noticed as her six-year-old son walked to the bus stop that his clothes were on backwards!). While we don't always have frazzled mornings or feel vulnerable, thank goodness, often enough there are plenty of reasons to feel guilty if we look for them.

Single mothers do have an "out" in this respect which we may take from time to time—sometimes quite justified, sometimes less so—that helps us avoid beating up on ourselves when things go wrong: "Well, there's only one of me; I can't be perfect." Married mothers have a bit more trouble with this one, because even if their partner is grouchy or unavailable after work, there *is* another person to share the work of parenting. This two-parent tag team approach can be helpful when we need to stay attuned to our children or on top of details that are important to their care and growth. We single mothers can and should accept our limitations and failings because we're human beings and because, indeed, we're single-handedly doing the work of two people.

Yet there are instances in which, for our children's sake as well as our own, we mustn't stop there. After we've allowed ourselves a "grace period" of sorts, it's wise to go a step further and analyze the situation to determine (1) what, if anything, we need to do now or in the future to repair or improve situations that resulted from our inattention or mistakes, and (2) what we can do to prevent or at least minimize the chances of those slipups happening again.

Encourage those who are timid. Take tender care of those who are weak. Be patient with everyone.

1 Thessalonians 5:14

Are you called to help others? Do it with all the strength and energy that God supplies.

1 Peter 4:11

Love is patient and kind.
1 Corinthians 13:4

God, please help me to notice and understand my child's needs in all areas of life. Give me the wisdom to know how best to meet those needs as they change over time; the patience and strength to take good care of my child even when I feel tired or distracted; and the clarity to know when I should ask for guidance or help from others. Amen.

10

Your Child's Behavior

Without a behavioral plan, parents can easily become too permissive, too strict, too laid-back, or too overprotective. It's easy to go back and forth between these extremes, and we've all done this from time to time. The key to success in raising an emotionally balanced, happy child who has good self-esteem and respects others is having a good behavior guidance system. Such a system has three primary features: (1) it teaches self-discipline; (2) its rules, consequences, and incentives make sense and can be maintained on a daily basis; and (3) it can be adjusted as our children mature and when new issues surface.

> Watch out for the most common triggers of a hateful outburst. Your child may be tired, hungry, resentful, or simply overwhelmed rather than genuinely angry with you. Consider whether a nap, a snack, a brief time-out, or maybe in some cases a snuggle on the couch may be all that's needed.
>
> Gail Reichlin and Caroline Winkler, *The Pocket Parent*[1]

Anna, a single mom with a busy career in architecture, asked what she should do when there's nobody around to back her up on discipline matters. "I see my married friends reinforce each other, and their kids seem to listen and behave better than my sons do. Sometimes I think I could lose my voice from all the repeating and ordering and threatening that I have to do to get them to cooperate."

Anna felt outnumbered. Her sons tended to "gang up" against her whenever she set limits, and while she always began by being calm and firm, she often ended up buckling and giving in or yelling in frustration.

"There are two of them and just one of me, and I really don't think my rules are unreasonable or unfair. My kids are spoiled compared to the way I was raised. They used to listen to me, but now that they're eleven and thirteen, that seems to be a thing of the past. What can I do about this?"

Anna thought that perhaps it was too late to make changes, but while it's more challenging with older children and teens, it's never too late to develop a good guidance system to encourage better cooperation and behavior. Her sons were doing what most children their age are doing—testing limits, questioning adults' decisions or statements, and thinking for themselves. This is part of the normal maturational process, but the needs of preteens and adolescents need to be understood. They need more choices as they get older, but their freedoms should be kept within reasonable boundaries.

Anna was fortunate to have children who got along most of the time, but this did result in her feeling outnumbered when they didn't like the limits she was trying to set. Being a single mom, she wanted to parent with confidence, but sometimes she felt both out of control and out of ideas.

It can be hard to retain the feeling of being in charge under these conditions. As single moms, we need a behavior guidance system that we feel confident is reasonable, fair, and growth oriented. Our system doesn't have to be complicated, nor should it require threatening, shouting, or pleading to implement. Our children need a strong mother, not a common enemy, a would-be pal, *or* a limp noodle.

Anna realized that she could and should take action to "reboot" the family system so that her sons recognized that she was in charge, that her rules were fair, that she was open to her sons' input—and that ganging up against her wouldn't work.

Though as single moms we ideally have good relationships and fun times with our children, we must, for their benefit and ours, remain the mom. If you are having difficulties in the area of behavior, make it a point to read books on positive discipline, consult with more experienced parents whose children seem well adjusted, and enlist help from friends or counselors as needed.

Anna set up a new "behavior contract" system that she and her children were able to agree upon. After several versions were discussed, reviewed, and edited after feedback, they all agreed to basic ground rules and reasonable consequences, as well as some incentives and perks to encourage more cooperation and mature behavior. Several books outlining the process of developing and using a behavioral contract, whether formally (written) or informally (discussed and understood by all), are listed in the Recommended Reading section at the end of this book.

Avoid Focusing on Only One Child's Behavior

If you write down rules for one child, you should write some for every child in the home, even if the other children are presenting no problems. Otherwise the rules will only increase the "problem child's" feeling of alienation. If he does ask, "How come George never has to . . . ," the answer can be, "You follow the rules we make for you, and let George worry about the rules we make for him." The rules are different for different children because of disparities in age, maturity, proven capabilities, and special needs. You will continually reassess the rules for all your children as they mature.

Kenneth Kaye, *Family Rules*[2]

**Tips for Guiding Your Child toward Good Behavior
and Self-Discipline**

- **Decide on the specific behavior you would like to change.** Don't just tell your child to be "neat"; explain that you want him to pick up his blocks before he goes out to play.
- **Tell your child exactly what you want him to do and show him how to do it.** If you want your child to stop whining when he wants something, show him how to ask you for it.
- **Praise your child's doing of the behavior.** Don't praise the child, but rather praise what the child is doing. An example could be saying, "It's good you're sitting quietly," rather than, "You are a good boy for sitting quietly."
- **Continue the praise as long as the new behavior needs that support.** Praise continues to restate the correct way of doing things.
- **Try to avoid power struggles with your children.** Using a technique like Beat-the-Clock when you want your children to get ready for bed faster, for example, will help you reduce parent-child conflict because you transfer the authority to a neutral figure, the kitchen timer (which turns a chore into a game).
- **Be there.** If parents are there while children are playing, they can monitor the playtime, help their children learn good play habits, and bring about improvement. If they aren't paying close attention, many behavior errors will go unnoticed.
- **Avoid being a historian.** Leave bad behavior to history and don't keep bringing it up. If a child makes an error, constantly reminding him of his error will only lead to resentment and increase the likelihood of bad behavior.

Adapted from Jerry Wyckoff and Barbara C. Unell,
Discipline without Shouting or Spanking[3]

Parenting the Way You Were—and Weren't

Conflicting discipline advice, which abounds in books and magazines, on talk shows, and on the internet, can lead to conflict and confusion for you as well as your child. Jumping from one approach to another also tends to result in inconsistent parent behaviors such as the "cherry-picking" approach, wherein we take the advice that is most similar to what we're already doing, reminds us of what our parents did, or suits our mood at the moment. Alternately, we may grab onto any discipline approach that seems to be the opposite of what our parents used when we were growing up.

The problem with spur-of-the-moment discipline that we haven't thoroughly thought through or matched to our child's developmental level is that while we may solve the current problems, we're not really *teaching* anything. With the cherry-picking approach to behavior management, we end up going in several different directions depending on the day, how our kids are behaving, and how we're feeling. If we don't have a system for teaching good behavior that includes helping our child understand the "why" behind rules and limits, we'll find ourselves putting out fires without ever really helping our child to develop and improve the self-discipline needed for success in school, work, and relationships.

In an effort to avoid "stifling the child's potential," or perhaps to make up for harsh discipline they received as children, some parents are hesitant to set limits even when the child is disrespectful or out of control. At the other extreme, some parents, lacking an understanding of even basic child development and psychology, develop a virtual addiction to punishment as the solution to every problem. In both of these disciplinary approaches, the result is a child who will be poorly prepared to develop healthy relationships, good goal achievement, and emotional stability.

One of the most ineffective parenting approaches is a combination of the overly permissive and the overly punishing styles, in effect an "angry-guilty cycle" wherein parents are very lax one

---

The Bright Side of Single Mothering

Your discipline and incentives system can be more to your liking, more consistent, and more cooperative with your child. You're free to change the system when your child outgrows some portion of it or when new problems or needs surface.

day and overly strict on the next. This is the well-known "inconsistency" that we all experience from time to time, and it's not a big problem if this happens infrequently. Backlash, in terms of poorly behaved, impulsive, or chronically angry children, results when parental inconsistency happens frequently or most of the time. Nobody intends to be inconsistent, but if we were parented that way and we've never really noticed the swings in our own behavior, we may develop this habit such that we're parenting by mood rather than by values.

As part of the inconsistency habit, parents will "lay down the law" and set harsh consequences, then feel terribly guilty and regretful, hoping to "make up for it" by becoming overly lenient. They then get upset when misbehavior gets out of hand, becoming too punishing again, and then "make up for it" once again by giving in or failing to firmly say "stop doing that" . . . and the angry-guilty cycle continues. This is the most common parenting trap of all. It creates a lot of wear and tear on us as parents and leads to many problems for our children.

The permissive-to-strict cycle is easy to fall into and requires a lot of parental reflection, rethinking, or help from others to break out of. But if you're able to see this pattern for what it is and are determined to change it, it *can* be done. Both you and your child will benefit enormously from getting free of this exhausting and ineffective cycle.

Our emotions are so tied up with our parenting approach because we feel we must either (1) be loyal to everything our parents did (otherwise we fear that we're saying they made mistakes) or (2) do absolutely nothing they did (fearing that our children will suffer as we did, we may toss out a few smart things that our parents did).

> Spare the rod and guide the child.
>
> Teresa Whitehurst, *How Would
> Jesus Raise Your Child?*[4]

If we want to provide the very best foundation for our children, we must step back, evaluate the short-term as well as long-term effects of the ways in which we were raised, and think more objectively about what we need to discard and what we should hold on to.

What we need is a value-driven approach to discipline that provides a solid, sensible framework for all that we do as parents to help our children develop into the kind of person we want them to be. I can think of no better value on which to base your discipline system than what Jesus gave us: "Do to others as you would have them do to you."

If It Ain't Broke, Don't Fix It

You've made it to adulthood and have developed the skills necessary to get along with others and to handle the responsibilities and challenges of adult life. Now you're a mother, caring for your family as well as yourself. Whether your parents were wonderful or troubled, obviously somebody did something right because you've evolved into a competent adult. You've probably noticed that you use certain parenting techniques that your parents used. Some of these techniques are part of the family legacy that you want to hand down to your children. No matter how unlikely it may now seem, take heart in knowing that your children will likely replicate your most helpful and positive parenting methods later on with their own children (though, be warned, they may never give you credit!).

These positive traditions and techniques for raising children have helped you as well as your family, and they are worthy of your gratitude and appreciation. Your parents may have been very affectionate, curious about the world, or fun loving. They may have modeled self-confidence and perseverance, a great work ethic, love for the outdoors, or compassion for others. In this age of looking primarily for the negative in our pasts, it's important to be able to recognize the positive—even if your childhood was a difficult one. It's uplifting to think about the positive, but more than this, it's wise to recognize what your parents did right with you. Don't feel that you must do *everything* differently, throwing the baby out with the bathwater because they made mistakes or failed you in some ways.

These, of course, are the parenting skills that you'll want to repeat. It's beneficial to share with your children that you're using a technique or approach that your parents used that helped you as a child. "If it ain't broke, don't fix it," as the saying goes.

But If It *Is* Broken, Fix It

However, it only makes sense that if something *is* "broken," you should do your best to fix it. Of course, changing inherited parenting techniques is easier said than done. Whatever you're used to is what comes most naturally, even if it has negative results. The brain is an energy-efficient organ that "unlearns" destructive patterns only when there's a pressing external need or if you have a strong internal intention to replace those patterns with something better.

Because there are many excellent books on positive discipline techniques (see Recommended Reading for some good ones), a full discussion of this topic isn't necessary here. However, you may find it helpful to consider the following goals and tips for guiding your own child toward good behavior, empathy for others, good values, and self-discipline. Some goals of an effective behavioral guidance and discipline system are:

- To help your child understand and manage his emotional and physical states
- To help your child accept the need to abide by adults' rules *without* feeling that he or she is "bad" in any way or that authority figures are unreasonable, uncaring, or unfair

- To encourage empathy for other people's feelings and needs (including yours)
- To provide reasonable limits and consequences that don't feel oppressive or lead to anger/rebellion but do motivate her to improve behavior and cooperation
- To provide an effective, positive model for limits, consequences, and incentives for improvement that your child will copy when developing his own self-discipline and inner dialogue
- To help your child learn how to balance her own needs with those of others
- To promote responsibility, perseverance, self-correction, and other skills necessary for school and work success

Tips for an Effective Behavioral Guidance and Discipline System

1. *Always give advance notice.* This is the most important principle of all, and if you get this one right, you'll avoid the unnecessary emotional reactions, rebellion, or passive-aggressive behaviors that so many parents find erupting as the child grows older. Using the advance notice principle, you let the first behavioral offense go, "issuing a warning" that the next such violation will result in a negative consequence, much as a traffic officer can write a warning rather than a costly ticket if you weren't aware of the speed limit or other traffic signal. When we are given a chance to correct our behavior, particularly when we weren't clear about a given rule or expectation,

    a. we feel that we're being treated fairly, and
    b. we learn and remember what the rule was and that we mustn't make that mistake again.

As single mothers, we certainly don't want to breed *more* problems—we just want our child to learn the rules and abide by them without a lot of fuss and without making him or her feel unjustly blamed or overly punished. We want our child to self-correct next time. If he or she fails to do so, we want to make sure that our child realizes what went wrong and accepts responsibility rather than simply getting mad at us. It's tempting, when your child suddenly behaves badly in some way you never expected—say, hitting another child or being rude to guests—to immediately impose consequences: "Okay, you're grounded for a week!" However, if this particular behavior never happened before, you'll help your child avoid this in the future if at the first offense you talk about the behavior, what led to it, and why it's not acceptable. By doing so, you're giving your child the benefit of the doubt by issuing a warning that if this happens again, a negative consequence will be given (specify what that will be—for example, no playdates or video games for a week).

2. *Give your child the benefit of the doubt.* While your child is more immature and has much to learn, he or she responds just as you do to rules and consequences. As described above, if you're slapped with a traffic ticket for a mistake you didn't realize you were making, you'll probably feel angry and will blame the person penalizing you for this surprise consequence.

3. *Don't set "speed traps."* The politicians in charge of some small towns have, as reported in many news stories, been found guilty of setting speed traps in order to generate income.[5] This trick, wherein a tiny strip in the middle of a 55 miles per hour speed limit road is designated 25 miles per hour without warning or obvious signs, is similar to what many parents do without realizing it: when tired, frustrated, or suddenly fed up, these parents will, without advance warning, punish their child for rules that he or she was not really aware of or that are so strict that it's difficult to adhere to them.

4. *Avoid screaming and spanking.* These behaviors put the focus on *you*, not your child's behavior. It's not only for your child's sake but for your own that I urge you not to scream or spank when he or she misbehaves. If you keep in mind that your child's cause-effect

150

reasoning and emotional responses are very much like your own, you'll naturally want to avoid yelling or hitting.

To use the traffic analogy once again, imagine what you'd learn if you were pulled over by a policeman who hit you or got red in the face, yelling at you for being "a bad woman!" or accusing you of intentionally breaking the speed limit just to embarrass or upset him. You probably wouldn't be thinking about your own behavior in order to self-correct in the future—"I'll be sure to slow down in this school zone next time"—you'd be focused on *him*, thinking, "What a jerk!" "He's scaring me!" or "He really *hates* me!"

5. *Add incentives and perks to your behavior and discipline system.* To encourage your child's growth and maturation, emphasize the positives *more* than the negatives with respect to behavior, rules, and consequences, and show them how improvements will benefit them. Just as you should give advance notice regarding "next time" when misbehavior or mistakes occur, you can enhance cooperation and the desire to mature by giving advance notice regarding the kinds of new behaviors or self-management improvements that will lead to increased privileges, freedoms, or other benefits for your child.

For instance, if school tardiness has been a problem and you want to stop micromanaging or nagging every morning, tell your child that getting ready for school on time without your input for a given period of days will result in her being given greater discretion and choices in scheduling her own morning routine or in after-school activities. After all, this is how we grow in our adult lives: we are very motivated to improve our own skills or behaviors when we know that such improvements will lead to greater freedoms or benefits and more rewarding experiences, in addition to increased feelings of accomplishment and satisfaction.

Your children are no different. Give them something to strive for! Incentives and perks for good choices and behavior teach your child that developing self-control and growing more mature is rewarding for *them*, not just something that adults demand.

Externally focused punishments, such as yelling, slapping, harshly criticizing, and spanking are easy to administer and require no thought or planning. Adults tend to accept however they were treated as children as natural or tradition. But those who seek to raise their child as Jesus would must question these traditions. Is hitting or yelling at a child any way to guide him or her toward the higher path that Jesus urged us to take when he taught the golden rule?

Teresa Whitehurst, *How Would Jesus Raise Your Child*[6]

It's important that we as parents do our best to do as Jesus instructed: "Do to others what you would have them do to you" (Matt. 7:12 NIV). When your child misbehaves or simply has a "meltdown," it's easy to either give in (too permissive) or lash out (too punitive) rather than putting yourself in your child's place to imagine what might help you to calm down or get his or her behavior under control. What really helps is to understand the many underlying goals of misbehavior (though of course your child probably has no real idea why he or she is misbehaving). These goals that you should understand include, according to the authors of the STEP program:

1. Attention
2. Power
3. Revenge
4. Display of inadequacy
5. Excitement
6. Peer acceptance
7. Superiority

For each of these goals, there are good ways in which you can better understand the underlying desire in order to help your child behave better and to teach self-control. Refer to the STEP books in the Recommended Reading section in order to gain some shortcuts that will help you, with quick and easy tables regarding your child's behavior and the feelings behind it, and to help him or her through it. By learning this you can help teach your child how to understand and better manage strong feelings in the future.[7]

We must respect and accept how far our children, particularly older children, teens, and adults, will follow us through that door of acknowledgement, amends, regret, and forgiveness. They may come a few inches, a few feet, or all the way through that door to reunite with us on the other side, or they may simply remain aloof. And all these actions can occur quickly or over long periods of time.

Acceptance is at the very heart of parenting a child of any age, particularly as they grow older and are influenced by their friends, their partners, movies, television, self-help books, and so on. Parents of older children, teens, and adults must master the art of giving without expecting back in return. Though of course we're allowed to hope, we should keep that hope on a low boil, not rushing the changes we'd like to see in our children or in our relationships with them.

Do to others what you would have them do to you.

Matthew 7:12 NIV

And you yourself must be an example to them by doing good deeds of every kind.

Titus 2:7

Filled with love and compassion, he ran to his son, embraced him, and kissed him.

Luke 15:20

A gentle answer turns away wrath, but harsh words stir up anger.

Proverbs 15:1

Lord, help me to understand my child better and to be reasonable and collaborative when explaining household rules, chores, expectations, and behavioral limits or consequences. Help me to allow my child to express feelings and have input into these matters so that good behavior and cooperation become mutual goals, not just my own. Please give me patience and wisdom to discern when hunger, fatigue, or frustration is getting the better of my child, of me, or of both of us. Amen.

11

Your Child's Father

If you're like most of us, when it comes to communicating with or discussing matters related to your child's father, you've at times said the wrong thing, said too much, or both. Most single moms realize this isn't good for the children and try hard not to say anything negative, whether to them or within earshot of them. This can be a challenge if he's been absent from their lives, has behaved poorly, or has failed to keep his promises. Even if we exercise perfect control after a phone call or visit and succeed in making no negative comments, our nonverbal behaviors, facial expressions, teary eyes, or exasperated sighs can give us away.

Let's face it: sometimes we just can't be the perfect mothers we'd like to be. But this is an area in which we can and should strive to do our best, which often means being kind to ourselves, keeping our child's well-being paramount, and realistically assessing their father's good points as well as his problems or limitations.

Robin, who worked in the financial sector, was concerned because Jonathon, her sons' father, frequently promised to take them places but arrived much later than promised or called at the last minute to say he wouldn't be coming after all ("Sorry, something came up"). Robin wasn't sure whether she should push their dad to be more responsible, thus risking greater tension, or let things go in the hope that he would notice how his unreliability affected the children.

"My younger son looks so sad, and has even cried on occasion, looking out the front window for his dad's car," she said. "This makes me absolutely furious, and I know I'm less than friendly when he does show up. This carries over to other situations; my attitude toward my ex has gotten worse because of this kind of hurt, which I can't explain away. Sometimes I just lose it and end up shouting or hanging up on him when we need to discuss visits, vacations, or child support. If I ever mention that he needs to be more consistent as a father, things really get heated.

"Jonathon says I'm a nag and a worrywart, and maybe I am, but the kids deserve better. He's not a bad guy in general, but he's clueless about the boys' feelings; he thinks they're less vulnerable than they really are. What can I do? I know they love him and he loves them, but these 'little' things are adding up, and I'm worried that their self-esteem is going to suffer because of his carefree, almost adolescent attitude since we became single again."

This is a vexing problem for single mothers who, whatever their feelings about their ex, want their children to have a good relationship with him. The reason it's so difficult to know how to handle is because such fathers may not be overtly neglectful or abusive. In fact they may be quite affectionate and loving when they're with the children, but their unreliability and "cluelessness" can indeed affect their child over time. Occasional tardiness, cancellations, or no-shows when a father-child activity or visit was planned may not be problematic, but when habitual, these disappointments can impair a child's sense of being important in dad's eyes.

What's essential in such situations is to keep your cool, put your children's well-being first, and resist the temptation to become accusatory or "lose it" with their father. When our children overhear or sense our disgust or anger with their father, this adds insult to injury when he has disappointed them. We want to protect their feelings, and this "mother bear" instinct is natural, but it can worsen the situation if acted on (trying to cut off or reduce contact with their dad) or expressed verbally (angrily lecturing or yelling at him).

This is where we really must be the grownup, which, while necessary, is tough and certainly not fair. We may need to accept the fact that our ex is behaving childishly and irresponsibly or otherwise acting like a bachelor without children and regressing from his previous level of maturity. The good news is that this is often a short-lived process that fathers self-correct over time. As moms we can accelerate this process by trying not to nag or criticize but to discuss our concerns with our child's father in nonaccusatory ways and to "catch him being good," reinforcing more sensitive and responsible behavior as a dad. He needs to know that his children care about his view of them and tend to judge the degree of his love for them by his actions.

After considering how the current situation was affecting her children and how her response to it might improve or worsen the problem, Robin made every effort to control her anger so that she could ask Jonathon for a few moments to discuss "some concerns I have about the boys." While he was initially a bit hostile to her concerns, eventually he agreed that he hadn't been as consistent as he'd intended. Because she'd phrased her concerns with the assumption that he would surely care if his children were suffering in any way, he recognized that this was having a negative effect on his sons. Robin had wisely avoided any blame or judgment but emphasized how much he meant to their sons and gently shared what she'd observed.

Robin also wisely limited her observations to obvious behaviors and reactions (for example, "I know you probably had no idea that it would affect him this way, but when you cancelled the trip to the park on Saturday, Robby had tears in his eyes"), not her own interpretations or catastrophizing (for example, "You were so selfish to cancel at the last minute like that!" or "Robby was absolutely devastated because of you").

If you have similar concerns and phrase them as tactfully as you can, yet your child's father doesn't agree to talk with you or gets defensive or argumentative, don't push it. Instead, ask for a recommendation from friends or your doctor for a good child therapist, and schedule a consultation without involving your child's dad.

Three Tough Questions Your Child May Ask after Divorce

1. *Why did you and Dad split up?* Avoid statements suggesting that you "fell out of love." Then children may think that it is also possible for you to stop loving them. Let them know that this can never happen. . . . Assure your child that a mother is always a mother and that you will always be there for them.

2. *Will Dad ever come back?* Hope is the magic that sparks everyone's life in a positive way. However, falsely suggesting that a father who has no intention of returning will come back or stating that you would like a father to return with whom you have no intention of ever becoming involved makes way for more loss.

3. *Can I live with Dad?* This question has a totally different meaning when asked by a toddler and by a teenager. Older children may be thinking about living with Dad when their values and life plan are in place and they are able to take care of themselves. But when a little one asks, try not to feel threatened or unappreciated. Tell your child that it's okay for him to think about living with Dad when he is older. . . . Again, a little bit of hope is a healthy feeling.

   Keep in mind, too, that you wouldn't be the first single mom to have adult children develop a kind of friendship with a long-gone dad. If this remarkable event happens, your strength and loving spirit, which has enabled them to forgive the past, has helped make their father some small part of their lives. What a tribute and a triumph for you!

Andrea Engber and Leah Klungness, *The Complete Single Mother*[1]

Collaborate with the therapist in order to determine how best to proceed. Very often an objective third party, particularly a therapist whose goal is to help the child, can help you get the other parent involved and guide you both to ensure that your child's needs are better understood and met.

When You're Upset with Their Father—and It Shows

As mothers we strive to protect our children and encourage, wherever possible, a safe and rewarding relationship between them and their father. But I'll be the first to admit that I'm only human, and so are you. If you and he once had a close and trusting relationship that came to either a grinding or sudden halt, you're naturally going to have strong feelings, particularly in the immediate aftermath of the breakup.

Depending on the circumstances of the breakup and the time since it occurred, you may feel abandoned, outraged, devalued, betrayed, sorrowful, or utterly lost. These are powerful human emotions that no one on earth can flawlessly conceal at every moment. Certainly it's best to try to keep your calm and to at least fake some good cheer when your kids are around, but there may be moments when even if you say all the right things, your children can see what you're going through.

Stephanie, a corporate attorney in her late thirties, knew that it was best to never "bad-mouth" her ex-husband Mark. Though she at times felt outrage, the emotions she experienced most of the time were not hostility and anger. The problem she faced was in some ways even more difficult to manage and conceal than anger: she was, quite simply, heartbroken. Despite her best efforts, it showed, particularly in the months following her husband's pronouncement that he'd "found somebody else."

Stephanie's husband had left the marriage after twelve years of being part of what she, their family, and their friends had considered "the perfect couple." The initial shock of discovery was followed by a prolonged period of grief at losing her best friend, coupled with a new and unfamiliar feeling of powerlessness. She would succeed at appearing cheerful for a few minutes or hours or even a day with her clients and co-workers and while spending time with her children. But as soon as she was alone, the tears started flowing.

Blindsided by the unexpected divorce, Stephanie had no desire to be a single mother and could barely believe she had become one. For quite a while she just couldn't accept this new reality. She emphasized to anyone who'd listen, "But I *loved* being married!" as if saying this would somehow allow her to go back in time and they'd all be together again.

Needless to say, Stephanie's children couldn't help but notice that she was suddenly unsure of herself and, under the surface, grief-stricken. While her parents and friends were very supportive, this didn't seem to be helping her to get past her shock and sadness. Stephanie bought several books on handling divorce and helping children through the process and scheduled daily time to read these books, to pray, and to reflect. This helped her to understand herself better, to let go of her old identity as "wife," and to forge a new self-concept as a single mother who would one day be happy and in a committed relationship again.

Taking the good advice that she read, Stephanie also learned to simply separate herself from the children when she needed a good cry, often taking a comforting shower to disguise her sighs or sobs. Once she felt better, she was able to "be there" for her children without having to hold back feelings, thus appearing more upbeat for their sake.

If you're newly separated or are still in shock about the breakup, you know how hard it can be to "act normal" when we're around our children. Until you've reached a new level of acceptance and you feel more stable emotionally, you may need to simply excuse yourself to another room to cry, call a friend, or express your feel-

---

Helping Your Child through and after the Divorce

Strive to avoid: Shutting down their attempts to talk about the divorce. Blaming the other parent when your children talk about the divorce.

Strive to: Allow your child to complain about the divorce. Give voice to what you suspect are his or her feelings about it: "I know it's hard on you to go back and forth," or "I know it's confusing having two sets of rules to remember," or "I know you sometimes feel like you have to choose sides," or "I know it's really hard on you that we don't all still live together." Allow your child to complain about your role in the failure of the marriage. (You will likely need a lot of outside support to get this one right.)

Joshua Coleman, *When Parents Hurt*[2]

---

ings in a journal. You may have to explain to the children that you're feeling a bit sad or irritated today (probably a huge understatement, but these terms will be less distressing to your children than the truth—that you're horribly sad or utterly furious).

With this caveat regarding your humanity and the impossibility of being perfectly calm and reasonable after a breakup, it's important to reassure our children about their father, about you, and about the family as a whole. Without saying too much about it, make clear that this is a grown-up problem that will get better over time. Emphasize that that neither the divorce nor your emotions are the child's fault. Let them know that they shouldn't even think about trying to "fix" what's going on.

The Bright Side of Single Mothering

If your husband tended to be irritable, depressed, or angry or had other psychological problems, the impact on your child (and on you) will be minimized or eliminated, especially if time spent visiting her father is limited. As your child grows older, she will know from experience on visits whether or not he's improved emotionally such that she could enjoy additional time with him.

In other words, *let them off the hook*, and realistically offer them a comforting perspective, the long-term view that young people have a hard time seeing without help: that this phase, as uncomfortable as it is, will pass, and that after a while you will all be happy once again. Tell them that you're praying for this to occur as soon as possible, and assure them that God wants the best for all of you.

A wise person stays calm when insulted. An honest witness tells the truth; a false witness tells lies. Some people make cutting remarks, but the words of the wise bring healing.

Proverbs 12:16–18

Putting confidence in an unreliable person is like chewing with a toothache or walking on a broken foot.

Proverbs 25:19

In everything you do, stay away from complaining and arguing, so that no one can speak a word of blame against you. . . . Let your lives shine brightly before them.

Philippians 2:14–15

Get rid of all bitterness, rage, anger. . . . Instead, be kind to each other, tenderhearted, forgiving one another, just as God through Christ has forgiven you.

Ephesians 4:31–32

Lord, sometimes I must pray for patience when communicating with my child's father, and I thank you for helping me to protect their relationship the best I can by not always saying what I'm thinking. When challenges arise, please help me to focus not on him or his problems but on nurturing positive feelings between him and my child. Amen.

12

When You're Tired and Tempted

Our brains have a protective function—when our circuits are overloaded with tasks, challenges, and difficulties, we experience fatigue, a sense of being time-pressured, and frustration. While we've learned to ignore (or try to ignore) these signs of trouble, it's important to remember they're designed to get our attention. When we find ourselves feeling pressured, we often develop shallow breathing, headaches, or trouble concentrating. We may feel unusually irritable or nervous or notice that we have a backache.

These and other symptoms of stress and fatigue, unpleasant though they are, can be used to help us recognize when we should take a break or at least promise ourselves some relaxation as soon as possible. These sensations are signs that we need to temporarily stop the action, stop trying to solve problems, and take a restful time-out.

If you push yourself (or are pressured by circumstances) for too long and too hard without a break or with unreasonable expectations for endurance or perfection, you'll begin to experience high levels of stress. If this happens repeatedly, you'll enter the unhealthy zone of burnout, which can result in physical as well as emotional harm.

On the other hand, if you start becoming attuned to your psychological and energy reserves, you'll begin to notice early on when you're in need of rest and rejuvenation. By paying attention to the first signs of being overly stressed or tired and taking steps to change what you're doing, you can prevent a negative impact on yourself or your children.

Larry, a wise friend of mine, once told me that he'd learned one important fact about himself: when his mood began to drop, he might not succeed at attempts to feel better at the time, but he could *always* change his environment. "If I'm feeling low at home, I'll go somewhere. If I'm at the mall, I'll go home. If I'm at work, I'll take a walk around the block. It's amazing how simply changing my location can lighten my mood."

A brief walk in the park or the woods can have a dramatic positive effect: the exercise, however mild, combined with the change of scenery will help your mind to recharge and begin to "click" again. But what happens when, due to the circumstances of your life, you're not easily able to stop the action, go for a walk, or take a needed nap? This is a common dilemma for single mothers with demanding jobs and schedules.

Amy, a certified nurse specialist whose job is very busy and intense, enjoyed her work and felt great when she could help someone. Her children, she noted, were generally quite cooperative and responsible for their ages (eight and ten), so she had no complaints in terms of behavior issues. Her primary concern was that the demands of her job had, for the last six months, begun to impact the rest of her life.

"I'm tired a lot, but more than anything, I'm constantly waiting for the next shoe to drop," Amy explained. "I'm on call several nights a week, which keeps me on edge. Sometimes I feel like saying, 'I simply can't do everything at home plus this job, so I quit, effective immediately!' But I know I can't do that. I feel trapped with all I'm doing, and I'm so tired of this pager. I'm tempted to drink after work on the nights when I'm not on call, but this backfires because I end up with a headache and can't be as sharp the next morning. Sometimes I'm tempted to just leave the children alone on a weekend night if I can't find a sitter because I so desperately need to get out. I know this sounds terrible, and I'd never actually leave them alone, but lately I'm wondering if I've got what it takes to be a working single mother."

While at the moment Amy was focusing on her feelings of burnout, without realizing it she was also describing many strengths and accomplishments: she had a nursing degree, she enjoyed her work, and her children seemed to be well adjusted. She had been given a lot of responsibility in her career; clearly her supervisors had a lot of faith in her.

What was of concern was Amy's feeling of being overwhelmed on a *chronic* basis, which is associated with that burned-out feeling. She had the intuitive sense that she didn't have the resources she needed to keep up with key areas of her life, despite being motivated to do a good job in all of them. From what she described, her job was challenging enough as it was, but the "tipping point" that was negatively affecting her mental (and potentially her physical) health was the overnight on-call schedule. This wasn't a realistic setup for a single mother of school-aged children. Something had to give.

When we experience ongoing, repeated stress from impossible demands, insufficient downtime, or both, it's easy to become self-critical or even defeatist. Amy's danger signs included thoughts about impulsively quitting or just leaving the kids alone to go out at night. These were indications that she needed to make some changes in her life.

Amy had no real intention of giving in to these temptations that were borne of fatigue and frustration. What worried her was the fact that these thoughts were even crossing her mind. Additionally, she was quite critical of herself, internalizing the blame for having trouble fulfilling an unrealistic set of expectations and demands. Again, something had to give. More to the point, something needed to *change*.

I reminded Amy that she is a smart woman, a great nurse, and a good mother and that she doubtlessly recognized these facts at some level. The challenge facing her was to figure out what to do about her situation and then muster the resolve to take action— action that would require a lot of energy up front and possibly an uncomfortable conversation with her supervisor. But as the CEO of her family, Amy needed to be realistic about her strengths and limitations, an essential step in learning to better advocate for herself and her children.

Speaking of temptations, inertia and sticking with the status quo are two temptations that we seldom see for what they are. We often justify inaction in the face of problems we need to address as "not rocking the boat." Single mothers are especially prone to this temptation because we're afraid of upsetting the delicate balance of our lives or of exposing our children to risk.

However, not confronting our limitations and letting unhealthy levels of stress continue over time constitutes a real threat to ourselves and our families. And that's even more risky. After Amy reflected for a few days on the factors that were most responsible for her worst feelings of fatigue, stress, and burnout, she realized that her day job wasn't the culprit—the problem was her overnight call schedule. Unsure how to address this issue without jeopardizing her job, she scheduled a few sessions with the company's Employee Assistance Provider to discuss viable options and to gain an objective perspective on this situation.

After stepping back to see the big picture, and with the support of her therapist, Amy began to understand that because she was a people-pleaser who wanted to shine at work, she had agreed when hired—despite her misgivings as a single mother—to the added duties and often sleepless nights involved in doing on-call work. She mustered up the courage to talk with her supervisor about this and was pleasantly surprised when she was offered a twice-monthly on-call schedule, rather than twice or even three times per week. With this change, Amy found that she was more motivated and enthusiastic at work and far more patient with her children at home.

Steps to Take When You're Tired and Tempted

First, analyze the situation. Keep a log for the next few weeks of your activities and your stress level. Note where you're doing well, where things are a bit challenging, and where you end up feeling depleted or otherwise at the end of your rope. You may find that you need to alter your schedule, get more sleep, or arrange for more child care to facilitate relaxation or more time with friends. You may need to talk with your boss at work about changes that could help you function more effectively, or you may need to look for another job.

Next, talk with people you trust about the kinds of changes that could reduce, if not eliminate, your chronic feeling of being tapped out and overwhelmed. This is one time when you definitely should invite the feedback of others. Like Amy, you may want to discuss your dilemma with friends or a counselor.

Even if you can't stop everything and take an immediate break, you can always pause for just a moment, close your eyes to block out everything briefly, and say a prayer for the strength, patience, and coping skills you'll need until you can fully address the problem. This momentary "pause, relax, pray" habit will help you to avoid burnout and develop resilience in the face of problems. It's wise to keep calming music or nature sounds on hand for just these moments (my favorite is a recording of mountain brooks rippling quietly over rocks) and to consciously invite God's love and nurturance into your mind and body.

When you initiate this "pause, relax, pray" time-out, it may feel a little scary at first because you worry that you're not paying enough attention to the problem. However, you'll become more comfortable with taking breaks if you promise yourself that you'll return to this issue later on. Be sure to follow through on this promise as soon as you feel better, and you'll find that you feel far more confidence in yourself. Greater self-confidence equals greater trust that when you need to take a break, it's okay: you'll address the issues as soon as you can and with greater brainpower and emotional calm at your disposal.

When we don't stop when stressed, trouble brews: we experience a sense of pressure, fatigue, and anxiety. Our bodies release a hormone called cortisol that serves to trigger our "fight-or-flight response," quickening our responses and alerting us to danger. This physiological stress response, which also includes rapid breathing and heartbeat, is a good thing if the stressor happens briefly and infrequently. But when we suffer *repeated* stress, we don't become more responsive, we become *less* responsive to important matters.

Even if you're just on your way to burnout, everything starts to feel overwhelming. Commuting and picking up the kids, getting groceries, settling fights, paying bills, trying to find car keys—

Avoid the Superwoman Syndrome

Too many women take pride in single-handedly managing the kids, their jobs, their house, an endless list of tasks. But excessive self-reliance breeds isolation, which can quickly erode self-assurance. Underearners are especially guilty. In my groups for underearners, I heard the same complaint innumerable times: "I've always felt like I have to do everything myself. I don't even imagine that there's help to be had or anyone would even want to support what I'm doing. That's why I've really appreciated this group. It lets me hear other stories, lets me not feel so alone, and I get feedback."

Barbara Stanny, *Secrets of Six-Figure Women*[1]

everything starts to feel hard. This state of affairs isn't good for your children because you can't be at your best. Kids being kids, they'll undoubtedly notice that you're stressed and tired. This is okay now and again, but it shouldn't be a constant concern which can result in your child feeling insecure and uncertain that you're okay and interested in them.

This feeling is your signal to stop, if only for a few seconds, to do a quick mind-body check. Have your breaths become shallow and rapid? If so, intentionally slow them down—slow your breathing with three to five deep, slow breaths. If your heart is beating too fast or too hard, slowing down your breathing will help your heart rate to calm down as well.

Next, notice where your attention is. If you're stressed, your mind may be stuck on a problem, flitting around rapidly on this or that aspect but not productively focused on understanding what's going on or on coming up with a solution. When we're stressed, particularly if it's been going on all day, all week, all month, or even longer, we may not even notice how fragmented our attention has become, nor how our coping skills have been fraying around the edges.

A stressed-out, all-over-the-place brain will have trouble figuring out what the problems you're facing really involve and thus won't be

---

Before You Snap at Your Child

Assess your current emotional state before you take on a problem. Sometimes, by just stepping back and admitting (to yourself, if no other adult is around) that you've had a bad day at work, you're angry at a neighbor, or something unrelated to the kids is really bugging you, can help put things in perspective. . . . Avoid pushing yourself "just one more time" when you don't have an ounce of strength or patience left. Admit to your own imperfections. . . . Replenish yourself with the things that give you pleasure. When you're in a happy place emotionally, you can "be there" more effectively for your children.

Gail Reichlin and Caroline Winkler, *The Pocket Parent*[2]

> **The Bright Side of Single Mothering**
>
> You can be more spontaneous. You don't have to consult with or get approval or agreement from anyone before going to the park or the movies or having a relaxed mother-child evening with children's videos and take-out pizza.

capable of devising several good ideas for resolving them. Being a single mother adds to the likelihood of suffering this universal state of "overwhelm" simply because you're juggling so many balls all by yourself *and* are responsible for the well-being of other human beings. Lots and lots of people have multiple responsibilities and multitask all the time. They too feel overwhelmed when it all gets to be too much.

The difference for a single mom is that in addition, you know very well that your children depend on you to be there for them. If you're continually stressed out, they suffer too. If it goes on too long, you will become highly reactive to stress—feeling anxious or hyperirritable, or trembling or practically panting—while becoming *less* responsive to the issue you should be addressing.

There's a big difference between a reaction and a response: reacting is controlled by whatever's going on that's stressing you out, while responding is more thought out and is controlled by *you*. It's wise to analyze what's got you so tired and stressed that you're tempted to fall apart or throw in the towel. What's important is to determine what you should do next, to take active steps, and to respond effectively to the stressors you're currently facing.

A Word about Dreams Deferred

Single mothers tend to be a bit more vulnerable than either singles with no children or married parents due to the need to provide for their children and the chronic inner fatigue that comes from postponing their earlier dreams and goals. For those who had children early, this is especially true because they went, in a sense, straight from childhood to parenthood.

Many married women who had children later in life have become single mothers by default, without sufficient advance notice to prepare for life after widowhood or divorce. Other moms lack adequate financial support and often feel they have no other choice than to grab onto whatever job security they can find. This realistic appraisal and the clinging to unsatisfactory jobs, neighborhoods, friendships, housing, and family relationships may be necessary at first, but my caution to you as you consider your long-term goals is this: *settling is habit-forming.*

You want the best for your children. You're willing to make any and all sacrifices for them. Admirable? Yes. But if your mind's default is "sacrifice" rather than happiness, you will eventually feel discouraged and may even lose your zest for life. Sure, you're making ends meet. You're doing what's expected of you. You're taking care of everybody and doing everything as you're supposed to do. But somewhere along the way, you've left yourself behind— the *real* you. After a while your dreams can begin to fade until you gradually become content with just getting by. If this happens, you don't even aim to be happy; you just want to survive.

The combination of feeling chronically tired and believing that your ship has passed may lead you to settle for whatever you can get. You may assume that you can't improve your life due to your obligations as a single parent, an assumption that is strong but subtle. Little by little your mind grows weary from routines and demands that never seem to change. When your mind gets tired on a regular basis, depression (even if low-level but chronic) sets in, and your body will almost certainly become fatigued as a result. Even after a brisk walk or a workout, you may still feel tired.

This feeling of fatigue is not psychosomatic. One of the primary complaints by people who've had strokes or other brain injuries is physical fatigue, which they assume is due to feeling ill or not trying hard enough to get back to their previous energy level. What they don't realize is that physical fatigue is a common consequence of stroke and other brain injuries. In addition, the person with brain injury must expend energy on the associated compensation required by other parts of the brain as it tries to recover.

If you feel physically or mentally fatigued on a frequent basis, do a self-check to discover how much hope you have for the future. If you discover that your hope has lessened or disappeared, it's time to take this seriously and get the help that you need. This may consist of an intense period of reflection and reading (see the Recommended Reading section for books that provide more than the usual self-help pep talk), or it may require professional help. You may need a supportive counselor, a hands-on practical advisor, or both. For some people, medication for depression, anxiety, or insomnia may also be very helpful.

Three things *not* to do if you've been feeling worn out, anxious, or depressed:

1. Don't be shy—ask for the help you need. If you don't have the money or insurance required, keep asking people for referrals until you find someone who can help you get this essential care. Your employer may have at least an Employee Assistance Provider available for you to talk these issues over with.
2. Don't let pride get in your way—as a single mother you may have gotten used to "Superwoman" mode, so this can be a real roadblock if you're not aware of your tendency to tough everything out in a stoic way.
3. Don't procrastinate when you feel your optimism fading—do something that will help you, even if it's just the baby step of calling somebody who might know somebody who could help you in some way.

If you've been stuck in a stressful rut or have been barely getting through life, take an aggressive approach to restoring your spirit, mind, and body. Even if you don't feel motivated to do it for you, *do it for your child.*

Pitfalls to Avoid

If you've been tempted to go too far in one direction or the other—that is, too much self-denial versus too much self-indulgence—join the club! We single mothers tend to swing between the extremes of overextending ourselves and melting into puddles of fatigue. We expend great energy in caring for our children and their needs, maintaining the household, bringing in the money, handling homework issues, coordinating sleepovers, and then this huge, ongoing outflow of energy leads to feelings of burnout and self-neglect. We may then experience that cheated feeling: "But what about *me*? Don't I get to relax and have some fun too?" For a healthier approach and for a more consistent energy level, we need to schedule in rest and renewal periods for ourselves so that we aren't caught in those extremes and can live with a greater sense of balance.

Single motherhood sometimes feels easy, like a breeze, when things are going smoothly. But sometimes when difficulties or a million little annoyances pop up, it starts to feel like a huge chore. Though we love our children dearly, we single mothers must keep our eyes on so many bouncing balls that we may find ourselves paying too much attention to this one or to that one, ignoring other important areas of our lives.

This is when we can learn to avoid falling into counterproductive or unhealthy patterns of thinking and behavior. What's best is to learn to recognize them early and take action to get ourselves on a more balanced, positive track. Consider the following common unhealthy thinking habits of single motherhood:

> A parent who is too busy or doesn't realize the importance of tuning in to his or her child often expresses surprise when the child gets into trouble or drops out of school. The child knows, but frequently can't explain, that those "bad kids" he or she hangs out with are like a lifeline. This is the secret pull, not the drug or the crime culture itself. Many young people have told me that they hated the filthy conditions or dangers associated with a drug or gang lifestyle. But for children who don't feel understood, all the unpleasantness and risk in the world is worth the feeling of being seen and heard by someone. Children need their thirst for attention quenched through strong connections with their parents. The connection between child and parent, if strong and consistent, paves the way for the child's lasting connection with God.
>
> Teresa Whitehurst, *How Would Jesus Raise Your Child?*[3]

- Focusing all your efforts on your child, particularly if that child is experiencing problems in one or more areas of life
- Trying to be Superwoman—the perfect mother, employee, sister, daughter, girlfriend, friend, and everything else rolled into one
- Keeping your nose to the grindstone with the idea that single mothering must be arduous and all-consuming, explaining to others, "I couldn't possibly take any time for myself; this is what I have to do"
- Feeling so deprived that you start saying yes to party or date invitations even when you have no idea how you'll line up child care for that evening
- Feeling such relief from having endured long periods of loneliness that you pay nearly one hundred percent attention to your new boyfriend, hushing the kids when they want to talk to you privately, join in conversations, or come with you on outings
- Getting overly tired and having an inadequate child care support network, such that you never get a break and you start

to (openly or subtly) show resentment or irritability to your children

- Taking every fussy period or moody complaint from your child to heart and assuming that he or she would be happy if only you were a better mother

Single-Mother Guilt and Worry

As parents we will all, sooner or later, feel guilty and worry. These may seem to be separate emotions and in a sense they are, but for those of us who are single mothers, guilt over past mistakes or for having "failed our child" in some way tends to rotate in a vicious cycle, leading us to worry about the consequences, which then creates more guilt. Sometimes we assume that by having made choices we later regret, or by not noticing early signs of trouble, we're bad mothers, that our child is ruined forever, and that we should feel very guilty indeed. This leads to even more worry about the past and the future and . . . well, you get the point.

Joyce Meyer urges us to stop the worry and hand-wringing in its tracks, both for our sake and for that of our children:

> Parents, teachers and other role models can teach children how to fear or they can teach them to be bold. A mother who is fearful herself will transmit that fear to her children. She will be overly cautious about many things and a silent fear sinks into the heart of her children. We should not teach our children to live recklessly, but we should teach them to be bold, take action, and to never be so afraid of making mistakes that they won't try things. I believe we should teach our children and those under our authority to take chances in life. If we never take a chance we will never make progress. . . . I encourage you to teach others by words and example how to be bold and courageous.[4]

Especially when you're tired and tempted, you need to schedule some rest for yourself and avoid falling into the trap of feeling anxious, guilty, or unrealistically responsible for every painful or challenging situation that your child or your family has experienced. We can't control everything that happens in our lives or our children's lives. Nor can we be perfect. What we can do is trust that God forgives our shortcomings and will help us to overcome them, if we will just remember to pray and to give our single-mom brains—which are all too often in overdrive—a rest.

Especially when our children are young, it's tempting to believe that we have to predict and solve every problem that comes along. But this isn't wise. We must remind ourselves that we are not the only influence in their lives. As the authors of *Parenting Young Children* note,

> As parents, it is important that we deal with our fears and insecurities about our children's independence. We can begin by recognizing *our* mixed feelings about control—is it possible we may want to keep our children dependent? For many years to come we will balance encouraging independence and setting limits. It's necessary to do both. As we encourage children to grow emotionally, we see that maturity and independence are possible. This can help us grow more secure.[5]

And as I wrote in *How Would Jesus Raise Your Child?*,

> I've worked with high-powered professionals who could buy their children every designer item in the finest boutique, but their children had become distant, depressed, or hostile. These parents first responded to their children's behavior by trying harder and giving their children pep talks or expensive presents. Yet the harder they tried, the more distant and ungrateful their children became! When I have spoken with children from such families, I have seen that they don't want more effort or more indulgence; they want more *parent*. It is hard to convince these over-scheduled parents that their children need a different kind of time with them; they believe in that mystical thing called "quality time."
>
> Searching for an image that would convey what their children most need—relaxed, long stretches of just-being-with time—I have

finally found one that works. It is the image of a whale, too large for quick turns or fancy moves, just drifting along in the deep ocean waters, her little one swimming with her, side by side, just doing routine daily things, taking their time.

Once these parents slow down, they realize that their children need more of *them*, but in "whale time." They learn to "clothe" their children with side-by-side attention and acceptance, and their children respond over time.[6]

It can be challenging to let go of our worries and guilt, but it's best that we do so regularly. Just offer them up to God, and leave them there. Remember, you're not perfect and you never will be, and neither will your children, or anybody else's children for that matter! Give yourself a break. By so doing, you'll be modeling the kind of healthy balance that you need in order to stay strong as a mother and be the model of courage and self-forgiveness that your children need to see in you.

But remember that the temptations that come into your life are no different from what others experience. . . . When you are tempted, he will show you a way out so that you will not give in to it.

1 Corinthians 10:13

O LORD, you have examined my heart and know everything about me. You know when I sit down or stand up. You know my every thought when far away. You chart the path ahead of me and tell me where to stop and rest.

Psalm 139:1–3

And don't let us yield to temptation.

Matthew 6:13

For when your faith is tested, your endurance has a chance to grow.

James 1:3

For I have given rest to the weary and joy to the sorrowing.

Jeremiah 31:25

Lord, when I'm so exhausted from all my responsibilities that I feel like throwing in the towel for a day, an hour, or just a few moments, please help me to feel your comforting, calming presence. Whisper, at those moments, that "this too shall pass" so I'll remember to take a breath and take a break, thus not failing my child or myself or making decisions I'll later regret, when I'm tired and tempted. Amen.

Conclusion

Taking Action for Yourself and Your Family

I hope that by this time you've been analyzing your life with the help of the Single Mother's Inventory, reflecting on which areas are and aren't going well. I hope that you're making the time, if only thirty minutes a day, to listen to music that calms you, to think, to read, and to pray for what you need. You may have a list of goals for improvement and may be consulting with others to determine the best strategies and next steps to get you there. All of these are prerequisites for moving forward. Be sure to praise and congratulate yourself on every step you take to improve your life and your child's life. Well done!

Once you've got a firm handle on what needs to be done, why, when, and with whose help, you're going to start feeling a bit impatient. This feeling will build gradually, and at first you'll notice it only now and then. But at some point you'll realize what this impatience signifies: you're ready for *action*. The planning has reached an adequate level, and you're feeling much clearer about

Go for it. Start. Make weekly and daily to-do lists, making sure you're reasonable in your expectations of yourself. Be forgiving and kind when a to-do didn't get done on the day you'd hoped. Simply move it to the next good day to take that action.

your challenges, goals, and dreams. Your mind, body, and spirit are poised for action.

Little by little, take actions that will address the issues that you've determined should be improved. Don't get stuck in the preparation phase so long that you begin to wonder if you're really serious about pursuing your goals. I'll confess, I often prefer the thinking and planning to the doing, especially if the doing is challenging or seems a bit scary at first. Even the most gifted people must make decisions, get feedback from others, and then take action if they want to turn their inspirations into real-life accomplishments.

I'll give you an example I witnessed decades ago that illustrates how important action is and how it can be far more important than talent alone. In a university creative writing class, I got to know a retired air force pilot sitting next to me. He was thirty years older than the rest of us and was taking the class "just for fun." While the other students came up with creative storylines, this gentleman always handed in stories on the same topic: tales of adventures with his military buddies in combat zones. I read some of them but got bogged down in the details of military life and found them pretty boring.

At the end of the course, my professor told me with a sigh, "That retired military guy will probably be the student who actually gets published." He explained, "There are more gifted writers in the class, but for them writing is just an easy class or a way to pass their time. But the pilot has a huge advantage: he's actually *writing*."

"What do you mean?" I asked.

I'll never forget his answer: "Natural talent for writing, like any endeavor, will get you only so far. Getting words down onto paper—that's the humble, unexciting *action* that gets a writer published." Sure enough, before the end of one semester, the pilot had found a publisher for a whole series of books describing his military adventures.

The takeaway lesson in this story is that after we've done our analysis, learned what we needed to learn, and sought out advice or help if needed, it's time to take action to better our lives and those of our children. Are *you* taking action in pursuit of your goals?

If so, keep up the good work! If not, begin today, even if all you can muster is squeezing in a thirty-minute break with your favorite hot beverage and some soothing music or your journal to begin acting on your goal of improving your self-care. Every little action counts and will give you more courage and motivation to take the next one. Whenever taking action becomes a bit over-whelming or you feel you don't have the energy to carry through on planned steps, take a break, reflect, and return to action once you feel renewed.

If you're not taking action to improve your life at this time—that is, if you're either doing nothing or doing only those things required to maintain (rather than enhance) your life or your children's lives, what's holding you back?

God treasures you and will be there for you every step of the way as you care for yourself and your children. I've been there, and I can tell you that when I forgot to pray for guidance and strength, it was easy to veer in the wrong direction, get overwhelmed, and start feeling that I was on my own without support.

God never meant for us to accomplish great things or even to get through the day on our strength alone. With our many responsibili-ties and our longing to do the very best we can for our children, we must pay special attention to our own spiritual development and cultivate the faith that when single mothers pray, God is always there for us and for our families.

So I say to you: Ask and it will be given to you; seek and you will find; knock and the door will be opened to you. For everyone who asks receives; he who seeks finds; and to him who knocks, the door will be opened.

Luke 11:9–10 NIV

Notes

Chapter 3: Single Mother, CEO

1. Chris Gardner, *Start Where You Are: Life Lessons for Getting from Where You Are to Where You Want to Be* (New York: Amistad, 2009), 29.

Chapter 4: Self-Care for Single Moms

1. Joyce Meyer, *The Confident Woman: Start Living Today Boldly and without Fear* (Bel Air, CA: Warner Faith, 2006), 232.

Chapter 6: Getting Organized

1. Gail Reichlin and Caroline Winkler, *The Pocket Parent* (New York: Workman, 2001), 219.

Chapter 7: Your Money, Your Job, and Your Dreams

1. Susan Reynolds and Lauren Bakken, *One-Income Household: How to Do a Lot with a Little* (Avon, MA: Avon Business, 2009), 38–39.
2. Ibid., 38.
3. Ibid., 39.
4. Gardner, *Start Where You Are*, 30.
5. Barbara Stanny, *Secrets of Six-Figure Women: Surprising Strategies to Up Your Earnings and Change Your Life* (New York: HarperBusiness, 2004), 210.

Chapter 9: Taking Care of Your Child

1. Teresa Whitehurst, *How Would Jesus Raise Your Child?* (Grand Rapids: Revell, 2007), 221.

2. See Jerome Groopman, *Second Opinions* (New York: Viking Press, 2000), 9–37.

3. Reichlin and Winkler, *The Pocket Parent*, 129.

4. See Don Dinkmeyer and Gary D. McKay, *Parenting Teenagers: Systematic Training for Effective Training of Teens* (Circle Pines, MN: American Guidance Service, 1990), 47.

5. Whitehurst, *How Would Jesus*, 196.

6. Ibid., 153.

Chapter 10: Your Child's Behavior

1. Reichlin and Winkler, *The Pocket Parent*, 153.

2. Kenneth Kaye, *Family Rules: Raising Responsible Children without Yelling or Nagging* (New York: St. Martin's Paperbacks, 1991), 37.

3. See Jerry Wyckoff and Barbara C. Unell, *Discipline without Shouting or Spanking: Practical Solutions to the Most Common Preschool Behavior Problems* (Minnetonka, MN: Meadowbrook Press, 1984), 3–4.

4. Whitehurst, *How Would Jesus*, 221.

5. "Tennessee: Speed Trap Town May Lose Every Speeding Ticket," TheNewspaper.com, June 11, 2008, http://www.thenewspaper.com/news/24/2418.asp.

6. Whitehurst, *How Would Jesus*, 218.

7. See Dinkmeyer and McKay, *Parenting Teenagers*, 19–20, 47.

Chapter 11: Your Child's Father

1. Andrea Engber and Leah Klungness, *The Complete Single Mother: Reassuring Answers to Your Most Challenging Concerns* (Avon, MA: Adams Media, 2006), 249.

2. Coleman, *When Parents Hurt: Compassionate Strategies When You and Your Grown Child Don't Get Along* (New York: William Morrow, 207), 165.

Chapter 12: When You're Tired and Tempted

1. Stanny, *Secrets of Six-Figure Women*, 193.

2. Reichlin and Winkler, *The Pocket Parent*, 332–33.

3. Whitehurst, *How Would Jesus*, 191–92.

4. Meyer, *The Confident Woman*, 182–83.

5. Don Dinkmeyer, Gary D. McKay, and James S. Dinkmeyer, *Parenting Young Children: Helpful Strategies Based On "Systematic Training for Effective Parenting (STEP)" for Parents of Children Under Six* (Circle Pines, MN: American Guidance Service, 1989), 138.

6. Whitehurst, *How Would Jesus*, 197.

Recommended Reading

For Getting Organized

David Allen, *Making It All Work: Winning at the Game of Work and the Business of Life* (New York: Penguin Books, 2009).
David Allen, *Ready for Anything* (New York: Penguin Books, 2005).
Erin R. Doland, *Unclutter Your Life in One Week* (New York: Simon Spotlight Entertainment, 2009).

For Understanding Your Child's Feelings and Development

Dorothy Briggs, *Your Child's Self-Esteem* (St. Charles, MO: Main Street Books, 1988).
Joshua Coleman, *When Parents Hurt: Compassionate Strategies When You and Your Grown Child Don't Get Along* (New York: William Morrow, 2007).
Penelope Leach, *Your Baby and Child: From Birth to Age Five* (New York: Alfred A. Knopf, 1997).

For Developing a Positive Behavior/Discipline System

Kenneth Kaye, *Family Rules: Raising Responsible Children without Yelling or Nagging* (New York: St. Martin's Paperbacks, 1991).

Jane Nelson and Cheryl Erwin, *Positive Discipline for Single Parents: Nurturing, Cooperation, Respect and Joy in Your Single-Parent Family* (New York: Three Rivers Press, 1999).

Gail Reichlin and Caroline Winkler, *The Pocket Parent* (New York: Workman, 2001).

Jerry Wyckoff and Barbara C. Unell, *Discipline without Shouting or Spanking: Practical Solutions to the Most Common Preschool Behavior Problems* (Minnetonka, MN: Meadowbrook Press, 1984).

For Insights and Strategies as a Single Mom

Andrea Engber and Leah Klungness, *The Complete Single Mother: Reassuring Answers to Your Most Challenging Concerns* (Avon, MA: Adams Media, 2006).

Jane Nelsen, Ed.D., Cheryl Erwin, and Carol Delzer, *Positive Discipline for Single Parents: Nurturing, Cooperation, Respect and Joy in Your Single-Parent Family* (New York: Three Rivers Press, 1999).

For Increasing Your Motivation and Confidence

Chris Gardner, *Start Where You Are: Life Lessons for Getting from Where You Are to Where You Want to Be* (New York: Amistad, 2009).

Joyce Meyer, *The Confident Woman: Start Living Today Boldly and without Fear* (Bel Air, CA: Warner Faith, 2006).

For Developing Better Skills and Attitudes Regarding Money

Dave Ramsey, *The Total Money Makeover: A Proven Plan for Financial Fitness* (Nashville: Thomas Nelson, 2007).

Susan Reynolds and Lauren Bakken, *One-Income Household: How to Do a Lot with a Little* (Avon, MA: Avon Business, 2009).

Barbara Stanny, *Secrets of Six-Figure Women: Surprising Strategies to Up Your Earnings and Change Your Life* (New York: HarperBusiness, 2004).

For Developing a Spiritual and Practical Parenting Approach

Michelle Borba, *The Big Book of Parenting Solutions: 101 Answers to Your Everyday Challenges and Wildest Worries* (New York: Jossey-Bass, 2009).

Stephen Covey, *The 7 Habits of Highly Effective Families* (New York: Saint Martin's Griffin, 1997).

Teresa Whitehurst, *How Would Jesus Raise Your Child?* (Grand Rapids: Revell, 2007).

Teresa Whitehurst is a clinical psychologist who provides counseling as well as personal and career coaching. She has worked as a psychotherapist for many years in private practice, at Harvard Medical School, and at Kaiser-Permanente. Dr. Whitehurst writes and speaks on parenting and personal development issues and is the author of *How Would Jesus Raise Your Child?* She is a single mom who has two adult daughters and two grandchildren.

Move from just getting through the day to getting the most from a day.

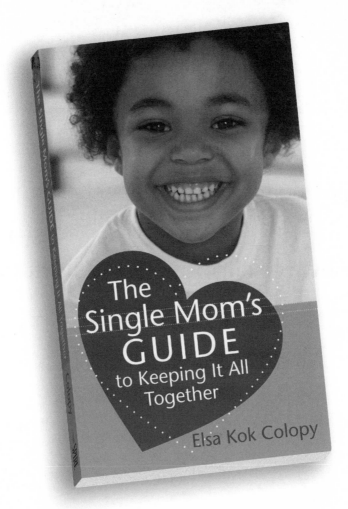

Despite the chaos of raising a family as a single mom,
you have what it takes to keep it all together—and enjoy it!

Be the First to Hear about Other New Books from Revell!

Sign up for announcements about new and upcoming titles at

www.revellbooks.com/signup

Follow us on
RevellBooks

Don't miss out on our great reads!